The New
Thanksgiving Table

An American Celebration of
Family, Friends, and Food

BY **DIANE MORGAN**

PHOTOGRAPHS BY **LEIGH BEISCH**

CHRONICLE BOOKS
SAN FRANCISCO

This book is dedicated to Greg, Eric, and Molly,
for whom I give thanks every day.

First Chronicle Books LLC hardcover edition, published in 2009

Library of Congress Cataloging-in-Publication Data available.

ISBN 978-0-8118-6493-0

Designed by ALICE CHAU.

Prop styling by SARA SLAVIN.
Food styling by SANDRA COOK.

Manufactured in CHINA.

10 9 8 7 6 5 4 3 2 1

Chronicle Books LLC
680 Second Street
San Francisco, California 94107

www.chroniclebooks.com

Acknowledgments

I give thanks to my family, friends, and colleagues, remembering and acknowledging our meaningful relationships and cherished friendships that make my life so special and every day a blessing. I have a long important list of people deserving of a big thank you. I wish you all could fit around my Thanksgiving Table—wouldn't that be a celebration and feast!

To Bill LeBlond, my editor at Chronicle Books, for all his expert guidance, support, and time. I'm thankful for this professional relationship and deeply grateful for our friendship.

To Lisa Ekus, my agent, for her amazing advice and enthusiasm. And to Jane Falla, Sarah Baurle, and everyone else at The Lisa Ekus Group for their dedicated support.

To Amy Treadwell, Peter Perez, Leslie Jonath, Amy Portello, Vanessa Dina, and the others at Chronicle Books, who have inspired, supported, publicized, and otherwise kept my projects on track. You are all delightful to work with. To Carrie Bradley, many thanks for copyediting my book with such care and precision.

To photographer Leigh Beisch and all the talented stylists, a huge thank you for your brilliant work.

To Cheryl Russell, my fabulous assistant, I'm so thankful for you. Honestly, I don't know what I'd do without you in the kitchen! We've tested and re-tested so many recipes, I can hardly keep track of how many books we've worked on together. You make developing and testing recipes a pleasure— even through all the many pans of stuffing, pumpkin pies, and pounds of turkey.

To my friends Harriet and Peter Watson, for your friendship and unwavering support. I can't hug and thank you enough. You bring me joy, sanity, and much laughter even when really big deadlines are looming. It is a delight to have shared so many Thanksgiving meals together.

Many thanks to my friends, family, and colleagues: David Watson, Paola Gentry and Eric Watson, Richard and Barb LevKoy, Larry LevKoy, Irene LevKoy, Antonia Allegra, Don and Joan Fry, Domenica Marchetti, Charlie and Jeanne Sosland, Bruce and Ellen Birenboim, Steve and Marci Taylor, Sukey and Gil Garcetti, Roxane and Austin Huang, Margie Sanders, Priscilla and John Longfield, Karen Fong, Sherry Gable, Deb and Ron Adams, Summer Jameson, Tori Ritchie, Josie Jimenez, Joyce Goldstein, Laura Werlin, Barbara Dawson and Matthew Katzer, Tony Gemignani, Braiden Rex-Johnson, Michael Wehman, Janine MacLachlan, Lisa Morrison, Marjorie Taylor, and especially Alma Lach.

To Adair Lara for her talent, humor, and time as the photographer for my author photo.

Finally, this book wouldn't have been nearly as much fun to write without my loving and nurturing husband, Greg, sharing in all I do. To my children, Eric and Molly, thank you for all your love, humor, and caring every step of the way.

Contents

An American Celebration of Family, Friends, and Food

Thanksgiving is my favorite holiday, no matter the season. Yes, that's season, not seasoning. Developing recipes involves countless hours, over many months, of cooking and tasting and writing. So there we were, my husband and I, enjoying an *al fresco* Thanksgiving dinner in May, followed by numerous other Thanksgiving feasts with family and friends in July, August, September, October, and—at last—November!

Writing a holiday cookbook is especially rewarding because holidays always bring into sharp relief the real stuff of life: breaking bread with family and friends, sharing traditions, and creating memories. Being surrounded by loved ones around a holiday table is truly an occasion for giving thanks.

My earliest Thanksgiving memories involve growing up in Pittsburgh, where by late October nature had cast off its autumnal finery, so the weeks leading up to the holiday were typically cold and gray. But then it was Thanksgiving, and my grandmother's kitchen was ablaze in harvest color, and the entire house was infused with sweet and savory smells of the upcoming meal. On Thanksgiving Day, the youngest children, including me, would furtively stick black olives on our fingers and then run from the relish tray with great fanfare to devour our treasure.

After completing *The Thanksgiving Table: Recipes and Ideas to Create Your Own Holiday Tradition* in 2001, I thought I had written my definitive treatise on the subject. But then I crisscrossed America for several years teaching Thanksgiving cooking classes, and I was regularly struck by the regional variations that give Thanksgiving tables in different parts of the country their distinctive character and flair. In many ways, this new book is rooted in those travels, with boundless enrichment from the wonderful people I met along the way—in Hartford, Phoenix, Richmond, Carlsbad, Houston, Austin, Cleveland, and Salt Lake City, to name just a few of the cities where I happily carved, brined, barbecued, roasted, spatchcocked, mashed, and puréed.

Thanksgiving is the one day of the year when nine out of ten Americans sit down to a home-cooked meal, and that meal, according to one survey, almost always features turkey. Depending on where you live, however, that turkey is roasted, smoked, grilled, deep-fried, or turned into the elaborate Cajun specialty known as "turducken," in which a boned chicken is stuffed inside a boned duckling, which in turn is stuffed inside a boned turkey, along with stuffing, to boot! There are also regional preferences in seasonings: sage and garlic are perennial favorites in some parts of the country, while rosemary, paprika, and cloves seem to rule in the South.

The celebration that evolved into our national day of Thanksgiving has its origins in 1621, in a three-day harvest feast that English settlers in Plymouth, Massachusetts, shared with the indigenous Wampanoag tribe. According to historical documents, that "First Thanksgiving" meal was based on New England fall harvest foods, including "seethed" (boiled) lobster, roasted goose and boiled turkey, rabbit, pudding of Indian cornmeal, seethed cod, roasted duck and venison, and a savory pudding of hominy, along with fruit and cheese. As the country grew, that menu expanded and changed to incorporate the ingredients of other regions and the traditions of other native and immigrant cultures.

The New Thanksgiving Table: An American Celebration of Family, Friends, and Food commemorates this quintessential American holiday with a spotlight on the regional specialties that make this vast land of ours so gastronomically amazing. While the classic Thanksgiving meal includes turkey, cranberries, pumpkins, and root vegetables, those same ingredients have been reinterpreted in myriad ways that reflect the diversity and breadth of twenty-first-century America.

Traditional cranberry compote, for example, may have Yankee roots, but it has metamorphosed into a cranberry salsa with onions and chiles in the Southwest. Or, the classic savory bread or rice dressings used to stuff turkey in the Northeast is often replaced with versions featuring crunchy, ebony-colored wild rice farther west in Minnesota, taking advantage of the native grain—actually a grass—of the region. In the Heartland, late-harvest corn is made into a pudding to accompany the holiday bird, whereas corn bread dressing and sweet potato spoon bread are served in the South. Along the Chesapeake Bay, a crab appetizer often starts the Thanksgiving feast, while along the Gulf Coast,

pickled shrimp or oysters on the half shell whet the palate in anticipation of the holiday meal.

The New Thanksgiving Table is filled with over seventy easy-to-follow holiday recipes. As in my first Thanksgiving book and my upcoming Christmas book, *The Christmas Table: Recipes and Ideas to Create Your Own Magic Holiday*, you'll find detailed sections on foods of the season, special ingredients, holiday equipment and tools, and menus and timetables to bring inspiring simplicity and helpful organization to your Thanksgiving Day. You'll also find stories, traditions, and facts about a particular regional ingredient or style of cooking. There's an occasional lesson in American history as well. For example, did you know there were two Thanksgivings in 1939? And, who was Sarah Hale?

Every recipe in *The New Thanksgiving Table* was family- and friend-tested, and most have cook's notes with details on ingredients and pertinent techniques and/or do-ahead tips about what can be frozen, how far in advance a recipe can be made and refrigerated, and how the recipe can be broken down into manageable steps. The goal is to have a Thanksgiving holiday that's delicious, heartwarming, and hassle free.

Even though the word "appetizer" was unknown to the Pilgrims, you'll find yummy ones here, including Vermont Farmhouse Cheddar Cheese Straws (page 24), Deviled Eggs with Capers and Wild Smoked Salmon (page 31), and Wild Mushroom and Goat Cheese Puff Pastry Pockets (page 35).

Mouthwatering soups and salads are plentiful, too, such as Butternut Squash Bisque with a Fried Sage and Popcorn Garnish (page 44); Oyster Stew (page 49); Hearts of Romaine with Crisp Red Apples, Celery, and Cider Vinaigrette (page 57); and Chicory, Pear, and Toasted Pecan Salad with Buttermilk–Black Pepper Dressing (page 64).

Of course there's an entire chapter devoted to the indisputable star of the Thanksgiving table, turkey, and its faithful sidekick, gravy. You'll find essential information about buying, brining, trussing, roasting, and carving a turkey. Gravy? Here are several that are fail-proof and tasty. So spend your holiday meal basking in compliments for Juniper-Brined Roast Turkey with Chanterelle Mushroom Gravy (page 82), Hickory Grill-Roasted Turkey (page 90), or Maple-Glazed Roast Turkey with Applejack Giblet Gravy (page 92), or a vegetarian main course: Molly's Pumpkin-and-Sage Lasagna (page 110).

Tease your palate with regional sensations in stuffings, casseroles, biscuits, and breads, including Linguiça Sausage Stuffing with Mushrooms and Caramelized Onions (page 119), Southern Corn Bread and Oyster Dressing (page 123), and Sizzlin' Corn and Jalapeño Bread with Bacon (page 134). Festive, brilliantly colored side dishes are here, too: Sweet Potato Purée with Pecan Streusel (page 147), Fresh Cranberry Salsa (page 161), and Southwest Simmered Green Beans with Garlic and Onions (page 151) number deliciously among them.

For some guests, the main event of the meal comes at the end with dessert! Reward their patience with Apple-Raisin Pie with a Pastry Leaf Crust (page 164), Spiced Pumpkin Layer Cake with Cream Cheese Frosting (page 167), Molasses Gingerbread Cake with Cinnamon Whipped Cream (page 175), or Indiana Persimmon Pudding (page 179).

One of the most wonderful things about Thanksgiving is that it's the gift that keeps on giving for several days. It's almost synonymous with leftovers! So have fun paying homage to the Thanksgiving meal by gobbling up the remains of the day in Cast Iron Skillet Turkey Hash with Soft-Cooked Eggs (page 196), Turkey Enchiladas with Creamy Tomatillo Sauce (page 205), and Classic Turkey Tetrazzini (page 201).

At the end of the book, I've included entire regionally themed Thanksgiving menus and timetables. Find that old recording of Woody Guthrie's "This Land is Your Land" and turn up the volume as you prepare a Thanksgiving Dinner in New England (page 212), a Heartland Thanksgiving (page 214), Southern Style (page 216), or a Bountiful Thanksgiving in the Pacific Northwest (page 218).

Here's wishing you a bountiful and peace-filled Thanksgiving—with a regional twist, of course!

The Autumn Harvest—Foods of the Season

Here's a list of seasonal foods and special ingredients for the recipes in this book. I provide tips on preparation, timesaving suggestions, and personal preferences for some brands and techniques.

BREAD CUBES Not all bread cubes are created equal. I like to make my own for stuffing—it's simple and can be done ahead—using good artisan bread. I cut the bread into ½-inch cubes, which I prefer to the typically smaller store-bought cubes. (See the following Cook's Note for baking instructions.) Dried bread cubes purchased from an artisanal bakery are my next choice, and commercially prepared bread cubes are an acceptable third option. If you purchase the latter, look for unseasoned bread cubes and packages that haven't been crushed, or you will have lots of bread crumbs instead.

COOK'S NOTE Making your own dried bread cubes is a quick and easy task with delicious results. There is no comparison between homemade bread cubes and the cellophane-packaged ones available in supermarkets. I usually prepare mine a day or two before Thanksgiving. Buy a loaf of artisanal or country-style white bread, trim off the crusts, cut the bread into ½-inch cubes, and spread the cubes on rimmed baking sheets in a single layer. Toast the cubes in a 400°F oven until just beginning to brown, about 10 minutes. Let cool completely and store in an airtight container until ready to use. Artisanal bakeries are springing up in every city and town around the country. Check out their breads for making bread cubes. If you are short on time, these same bakeries often sell toasted bread cubes made from their day-old loaves, especially during the holidays.

BRUSSELS SPROUTS Cute, like miniature cabbages, Brussels sprouts are typically sold loose, but some markets, especially farmers' markets, sell them on the stalk. Look for tightly packed heads with fresh green leaves, and avoid those with leaves that are yellowed or speckled with black spots.

CHESTNUTS Fresh chestnuts are always in the market by Thanksgiving. They are fun to roast and delicious to eat, but tedious to peel. There are about 3 dozen chestnuts in a pound, yielding about 2½ cups of peeled nuts. I often buy peeled chestnuts in vacuum-sealed packages, cans, or jars (see Cook's Note on page 55) for use in soups, stuffings, and the like. They are a time-saver, though not a money-saver.

CHICKEN STOCK AND BROTH I'm one of those cooks who always has homemade chicken stock in the freezer. It's a habit: Every time I roast a whole chicken, I make a small batch of stock by tossing the neck, giblets, and wing tips into a saucepan with a bit of chopped yellow onion, celery, and carrot; a small bay leaf; a few black peppercorns; and cold water to cover. I simmer it for an hour, strain it, let it cool, skim off the fat—and I have stock. It's easy and never feels like a chore—at least to me. Canned broth is a good substitute. Look for a brand that is low in salt; I prefer Swanson's low-sodium, fat-free organic broth.

CRAB There are lots of varieties of crab, both fresh- and saltwater, and what is available in your fish market will largely depend on where you live. In the Pacific Northwest, I mostly see Dungeness, which is prized for its sweet, succulent flesh. King crab and snow crab are also found in the northern Pacific. In the East and South, blue crab, rock crab, and stone crab are most readily available. For the recipes in this book, I used fresh-cooked lump or flaked meat from the body and/or claws (depending on the variety), which is readily available cleaned and cooked at high-quality markets and fishmongers. It's expensive, but also the tastiest, and is much preferred over canned crabmeat.

CRANBERRIES These are the small, red, tart berries of a plant that grows in bogs on low, trailing vines. They come in 12-ounce packages—look for bright red, firm berries—and are always available fresh at Thanksgiving. Check the recipe carefully to see how much you need, and buy extra bags for the freezer. A 12-ounce package is equivalent to about 3 cups. Cranberries are delicious in muffins, scones, and coffee cakes.

FLOUR The recipes in this book call for either cake flour, all-purpose flour, or Southern self-rising flour. I used Softasilk brand cake flour or Gold Medal unbleached all-purpose flour to test my recipes. (See the headnote on page 132 for information on Southern flour.) What is most important about flour when baking, however, is not the brand, but how the flour is measured. The proper way to measure flour is to spoon it into a dry measuring cup and level off the top with the blunt side of a table knife. Scooping flour right from the bag or from a canister with a measuring cup and then leveling off the excess means the flour is more compacted, which I find results in a less tender cake, cookie, or pastry. Weighing flour yields the most accurate measure, but because most American home bakers rely on volume measures, recipes do not typically include weights. If you like to use a scale, then use the following conversions:

1 cup unsifted all-purpose flour = 5 ounces
1 cup sifted all-purpose flour = 4 ounces
1 cup unsifted cake flour = 4 ounces
1 cup sifted cake flour = 3 ounces

NUTS Nuts are used extensively during the holiday season in both savory and sweet dishes. Store raw nuts in a tightly sealed container in the freezer to keep them as fresh as possible. Toasting nuts brings out their delicate flavor and makes any dish to which they are added more delicious; it is worth the minimal extra effort. (See the Cook's Note on page 60 for toasting directions.) If you need ground nuts for a recipe, you can purchase them already ground or buy shelled nuts and grind them at home in a food processor fitted with the metal blade, using the pulse button to control the coarseness.

OYSTERS Three primary species of oysters are sold in the United States, whether naturally grown or cultivated in oyster beds: Pacific, or Japanese, oysters, found on the Pacific seaboard; eastern, or Atlantic, oysters, from the Atlantic seaboard;

and the small and delicious Olympia from Washington's Puget Sound. Fresh oysters are available year-round, debunking the myth that you should eat oysters only during months spelled with an r. Quick processing and advanced refrigeration in trucking and storage keep the oysters fresh even during hot weather. However, experts think the best time to eat oysters raw is in the fall and winter because they spawn during the summer and the meat tends to be softer. I use fresh, shucked oysters that I buy from my fishmonger; you can also find them at high-quality and gourmet markets. The best are sold in clear, screw-top jars or in plastic pint and quart tubs so you can see that the oysters are tightly packed and plump, and have good color, and that the oyster liquor is clear, not cloudy. Ask to smell the oysters if you question their freshness. They should smell sweet and briny fresh, not fishy at all.

PARSNIPS Cultivated in Europe since ancient times, parsnips were brought to America in the 1600s. Resembling a carrot, this creamy white root vegetable has a complex sweet, herbal, and earthy flavor. Parsnips are available year-round, but their flavor is best in the fall and winter. Look for well-shaped, medium-sized roots that are firm with no spots or shriveled skin and no sprouting at the top. Store and cook parsnips as you would carrots; they are delicious roasted, braised, steamed, or boiled for mashing.

PEARL ONIONS These tiny, papery white or yellow onions are used in side dishes, soups, and stews. They are more flavorful when fresh, but frozen peeled pearl onions, available in bags in the freezer section at the market, will do in a pinch.

PERSIMMONS Bright orange with a smooth skin, persimmons need time to ripen. You'll most likely see two Japanese varieties in the market: The Fuyu is bright orange, squat, and tomato shaped; it is still firm with a nice bit of crunch when ripe and can be sliced and eaten like a tomato. The Hachiya is heart-shaped with a pointed bottom and has a smooth, bright orange-red skin. It has a very astringent taste when not ripe and needs to feel almost feel like mush before it is ready to eat. Persimmons are in season in the late fall. You can buy Hachiyas in quantity, allow them to ripen on your countertop, and then scoop the soft, jelly-like flesh from the skin and purée and freeze it. Persimmon pudding is a fond holiday dessert for many.

POMEGRANATES The pomegranate, one of only seven fruits mentioned in the Old Testament, is round, about the size of a large orange, and has a smooth, glossy red to red-pink skin that looks and feels leathery. Inside is a complex set of compartments made up of tiny, shiny, ruby-like fleshy edible seeds surrounded by spongy, bitter, cream-colored membranes. The seeds are the only edible part of the fruit.

To extract the seeds from a pomegranate, I suggest you wear an apron and disposable surgical gloves because the juice stains both hands and clothing. To remove the seeds, place a bowl of cool water in the sink. Cut off the crown of the pomegranate with a stainless-steel knife (a carbon-steel knife can turn the juice bitter) and scoop out some of the center membrane, or pith, with a spoon. Use the knife to score the skin into quarters, and then cut through enough of the membrane to see the seeds. Submerge the pomegranate in the water and break apart the quarters with your thumbs. Use your fingers to peel away the white membrane and pop out the seeds. The seeds will sink to the bottom of the bowl and the membrane will float to the top. Discard the membrane. Drain the seeds and spread them on a double thickness of paper towels to absorb the excess moisture. They are now ready to use.

SALT I keep several types of salt in my kitchen. Within easy reach of my stove and prep counter is one bowl full of kosher salt and another filled with fine sea salt. I buy Diamond Crystal kosher salt, in the red box, found at specialty-foods markets and many supermarkets. The sea salt I use is from the Mediterranean. Ordinary table salt includes anti-caking agents that leave a chemical aftertaste, so I don't use it in my kitchen. At the table, I offer a finishing salt, such as *fleur de sel* (a delicately gray, coarse-grained sea salt from France), for sprinkling on foods. I always use Diamond Crystal kosher salt for brining.

SHRIMP In the United States, shrimp is the most popular food from the sea. The sweet crustacean is divided into two broad categories, warm-water shrimp and cold-water shrimp. Within those categories are hundreds of species. From the cold northern waters come the small shrimp often referred to as bay shrimp. The most common shrimp from warm waters include Gulf, or Mexican, whites and pinks; Gulf browns; tiger shrimp; and rock shrimp. Shrimp are marketed according to size and are named to indicate the number per pound, for example jumbo (11–15), extra-large (16–20), large (21–30), medium (31–35), and small (36–45). Regardless of size, raw shrimp are typically sold either in their shells with the tails attached and the heads removed, or peeled and deveined. They are also marked either fresh or frozen. However, unless you are buying shrimp right off a boat or from a water-filled tank, almost all shrimp have been processed and flash frozen, because they deteriorate quickly after harvesting. So, "fresh" shrimp in the market have actually been thawed prior to sale. Buy shrimp that glisten and smell clean, fresh, and "of the sea." If you smell any hint of ammonia it means the shrimp are old and deteriorating. I prefer to buy my shrimp uncooked with the shell on. Cooking shrimp in the shell is easy and the results are more flavorful.

SWEET POTATOES AND YAMS Confusion reigns in the grocery store when it comes to sweet potatoes and yams. Technically, true yams are a thick, starchy tuber native to Africa, Asia, and many parts of the Caribbean. They are unrelated to potatoes, including sweet potatoes, which are roots, not tubers. Yams are mostly found in Asian grocery stores, rarely in traditional American markets. When you shop for sweet potatoes in an average supermarket in this country, you'll typically find two types: the yellow-fleshed variety labeled "sweet potatoes" and the dark-skinned, dark-orange-fleshed variety often labeled "yams" or "garnet yams." Those dark-skinned ones are technically sweet potatoes, too, and are mostly grown in North Carolina and Louisiana. The two types can be used interchangeably; however, the orange-fleshed sweet potatoes are higher in beta-carotene and sugar, giving a sweeter more caramelized flavor to the finished dish. Their yellow-fleshed counterparts are higher in starch, so they are better for baking. For the recipes in this book, I prefer the dark orange garnets.

WILD RICE Long considered the "caviar of grains," wild rice is native to North America and, despite the name, is not a true rice. The grains are long, slender, and black, with a unique nutty, almost smoky flavor. They come from a reedlike aquatic plant that was found only in the wild until relatively recently but nowadays is naturally cultivated. Local Native Americans still gather wild rice by hand, paddling their canoes through the rice beds of Minnesota. Wild rice is also grown in the southern states and in rural mountain valleys in Northern California.

WINTER SQUASH These types of squash are allowed to mature on the vine and are stored for use in winter. The skin is hard and inedible, and the flesh needs to be cooked before eating. Hubbard, butternut, pumpkin, delicata, and acorn are some of the more common winter squashes in the market.

Holiday Equipment and Tools

Cooking for Thanksgiving doesn't require a lot of fancy equipment, but some kitchen items will make your life easier and your cooking more pleasurable. Following is a list of the tools and equipment I used in making the recipes in this book.

For the Turkey

BULB BASTER This tool certainly makes basting meat and poultry easier, but a large spoon will work in a pinch. Buy either a stainless-steel or a heat-resistant plastic baster. I prefer the latter because I can see through it. Glass basters are a mistake—they inevitably break.

CARVING BOARD Different from a cutting board, a carving board has a "moat" that collects meat juices and a "well" that traps them. This is handy for carving all kinds of meats and poultry. My favorite type is a wooden board that is reversible, so you can use the flat side for chopping and dicing.

CARVING KNIFE AND FORK A carving set is lovely if you are presenting a whole bird and carving it at the table. A set is not critical, but if you don't have one, it is important to have a very sharp utilitarian carving knife and carving fork. After working hard to roast your holiday turkey, you want to cut smooth, even slices. A good knife is a lifetime investment.

FINE-MESH SIEVE Because a fine-mesh sieve can serve double-duty for cooking and baking needs, I stock my kitchen with three sizes. I use the large or medium sieve for straining stocks, soups, or sauces. I use the small one for dusting confectioners' sugar over cakes, pastries, and tarts. Medium-mesh sieves are also available and can be used for straining stocks; just be sure to buy a sturdy, well-constructed sieve.

GRAVY STRAINER This useful tool looks like a measuring cup with a spout that originates near the bottom. You pour in pan juices or gravy, the fat naturally rises to the top, and the relatively fat-free liquid that settles to the bottom is easily poured out through the spout.

KITCHEN TWINE Buy the proper twine to truss your bird. It should be 100 percent linen, which resists charring. Flimsy string won't do, and dental floss (I've seen it used!) chars and can tear the skin. You'll be surprised how often you reach for twine once it's in the kitchen.

MEAT THERMOMETER An instant-read thermometer, built with a small dial and thin shaft with a piercing end, is the most accurate way to judge the doneness of meats, poultry, and fish. Simply inserting it in the food for a few seconds allows it to register the internal temperature, which is an exceptionally accurate gauge of desired doneness. Note, these thermometers are not meant to be left in the food or the oven. For safety and sanitation, always wash the thermometer after each test. I prefer an analog thermometer to a digital one, as the readings on the digital models seem to jump wildly from one temperature to another.

OVEN THERMOMETER If you doubt the accuracy of your oven's thermostat, buy an oven thermometer before you start cooking and baking. Once you know how far off the thermostat is, you can adjust the temperature dial accordingly. Whether your oven is old or brand-new, it doesn't hurt to have an oven thermometer to double-check its accuracy.

PROBE THERMOMETER This thermometer is made up of a probe with a thin wire connected to a transmitter. You insert the probe into the food, put the transmitter on the counter next to the oven, and program the transmitter with the desired temperature. The newest versions have a transmitter and wireless remote, so you can walk up to 120 feet away and the pager will beep when the food is done. These thermometers are nifty, but consumer reviews have been mixed. If you like reading manuals and figuring out how to program gadgets, this is the tool for you.

ROASTING PAN These are usually about 4 inches deep and made of stainless steel or aluminum, sometimes in a nonstick finish (which makes for easy cleanup). The best ones are extra heavy and have sturdy, upright handles. Measure your oven before you buy! A medium pan, about 16 by 12 by 5 inches, is adequate for a turkey weighing up to 20 pounds. The best pans cost about $100 and will last a lifetime, but for years I managed with a black-and-white speckled, enamel-coated steel pan I bought at a hardware store for under $20. I don't recommend using disposable foil pans, except for grilling, because they buckle easily. If you must use them, buy two for double thickness.

ROASTING RACK A V-shaped steel rack, preferably nonstick, elevates poultry and roasts for faster cooking and keeps the pan drippings away from the meat, thus promoting crispy skin. Buy one with tall, vertical handles on each end; they make the lifting much easier. Non-collapsible V-shaped racks are by far my favorite. A high-quality, medium rack costs about $20. Before you buy, make certain the rack fits inside your roasting pan!

SERVING PLATTERS When you are serving a whole turkey, it is important to make sure you have a platter large enough to accommodate it. You don't need to spend a fortune for a china platter. Shop at outlet stores and discount shops, where you can have fun mixing and matching serving pieces.

For Soups, Salads, and Side Dishes

BAKING DISHES Count how many baking dishes you'll need for your planned menu. I usually need at least three 9-by-13-inch baking dishes or pans. The classic clear-glass dishes are great, though I prefer the look of white porcelain baking dishes. There are lots of attractive possibilities on the market, and they vary in price. Buy what fits your budget.

DUTCH OVEN I get my upper-body workout when I lift my 6-quart Dutch oven made of enameled cast iron. That heft is what makes it a great pot. Look for a Dutch oven with a tight-fitting lid and a heavy, flat bottom. Because Dutch ovens can be used both on the stove top and in the oven, they are the ideal pan for soups, stews, and braises like short ribs and brisket.

GRATERS, PEELERS, ZESTERS, AND JUICERS All of these handy tools make cooking and baking a lot more fun. If you don't own a rasp-like zester by Microplane, buy one. This is one of my favorite kitchen gadgets—it outperforms other tools for zesting citrus and works beautifully for grating whole nutmeg and Parmesan cheese. I prefer two-piece juicers, either manual or electric, because the cup part catches the juice and makes it easier to measure. The best peelers are the ones that have a serrated edge; they stay sharp much longer than the smooth-bladed ones. Buy a sturdy box grater, preferably made of stainless steel, and one that has a rounded and comfortable handle to hold.

MIXING BOWLS I use a steady supply of mixing bowls while cooking and baking for the holidays. My favorites are nesting stainless-steel sets, though I also have a set of glass ones to use in the microwave. Stainless-steel bowls are inexpensive, easy to wash, and last a lifetime. Buy several in each size.

POTATO RICER, POTATO MASHER, OR FOOD MILL If mashed potatoes or yams are on your holiday menu, you need to have a ricer, masher, or food mill on hand. Food mills and ricers are the best tools for lump-free potatoes. The advantage of owning a food mill is that it is also great for puréeing fruits and vegetables; Foley makes a sturdy one. The old-fashioned masher produces a coarser mash. (If you are contemplating using a food processor, don't. You'll end up with potato glue.)

SAUTÉ PANS AND SKILLETS When cooking for the holidays, I most often reach for my 12- and 14-inch sauté pans. Sautéing vegetables for a crowd requires a big pan, and the 14-inch size is ideal. Buy sauté pans that come with lids and have oven-proof handles, so you can also use them to make frittatas and other dishes that finish under the broiler. I use my 10-inch sauté pan for sautéing aromatics. As for skillets, it helps to have a variety of sizes and finishes. Cast iron is ideal when you want beautifully browned, seared foods. When I need pans with a nonreactive finish, for cooking acidic foods such as tomatoes that would react with an aluminum or cast iron surface, I reach for my All-Clad three-ply stainless-steel pans with an aluminum core.

STOCKPOT This large, narrow pot with tall sides is used for making soups and stocks. I own a 12-quart, multiuse stockpot with a shallow steamer pan and a strainer insert for cooking pasta. Three-ply stainless-steel stockpots with an aluminum core are terrific for even heating and slow simmering, but they are expensive and best as an investment if you foresee lots of use. An inexpensive aluminum stockpot works well, too, as long as the stocks don't contain an acidic ingredient, such as tomatoes or citrus juice.

TONGS Tongs are an essential tool for turning foods and for moving them around in a pan. They should be about 10 inches long, sturdy, stainless steel, and ideally spring loaded. I like tongs that lock in a closed position for easy storage, have comfortable cushioned, nonslip handles, and are rounded, rather than serrated, at the top.

WHISKS Whisks are indispensable for mixing sauces and salad dressings, whipping heavy cream for a dessert, and the like. Stainless-steel wire whisks are best because they won't rust. Whisks come in myriad shapes and sizes, but I find my 8-inch and 12-inch standard whisks the handiest. Balloon whisks are ideal for whipping egg whites, though a standard whisk will work almost as well.

For Baking

BAKING SHEETS I couldn't survive without my heavy, rimmed, nonstick aluminum baking sheets. They are workhorses in my kitchen for baking cookies, pastries, breads, crackers, and more. I buy rimmed baking sheets as opposed to rimless cookie sheets because they offer the most versatility. Use a silicone heatproof spatula to lift baked items, so you don't scratch the surface of the pan.

BUNDT PAN A Bundt pan is a tube pan with fluted or scalloped sides. The term *Bundt* is a registered trademark for a pan created in 1950 by H. David Dalquist, the founder of Nordic Ware. Bundt pans are made of cast aluminum and have a nonstick finish. A 12-cup pan is the standard size for most cake recipes. Cakes made in the new silicone tube pans don't bake as evenly or brown as well as they do in this classic pan.

CAKE PANS I own three 9-inch aluminum cake pans with 2-inch sides. This is the standard size for making most layer cakes. I prefer nonstick cake pans because the sides and bottom of the cakes brown evenly without darkening and forming a crust. In addition, most cake recipes suggest greasing the pan, lining the bottom with parchment paper, and then dusting the pan with flour. This guarantees the cake will release from the pan without sticking.

FOOD PROCESSOR A food processor is a time-saver all the time, but especially during the holidays, when we're often making pastry dough; pâtés, dips, and other spreads and purées; and redoubling our general chopping, grinding, and slicing. I prefer the KitchenAid processor because the lid's safety mechanism is much simpler to use and clean. Unless you like to use a food processor to make bread dough, you don't need a giant machine. The standard 11-cup model is what I have always owned and meets my preparation needs. A mini food processor is handy for chopping ginger, garlic, and similar items.

MUFFIN PANS For the Hazelnut and Fresh Herb Popovers (page 137), you will need a standard 12-cup muffin pan. I have a nonstick muffin pan made by Chicago Metallic and find it performs much better than older aluminum ones.

PARCHMENT PAPER AND NONSTICK BAKING LINERS I recommend using nonstick baking sheets, or lining a baking sheet with either parchment paper or with a nonstick baking liner—Silpat is the best-known brand—to create an excellent nonstick surface. Parchment paper is less expensive, but with care, the good-quality nonstick baking liners will last for years.

PASTRY BRUSH Natural-bristle brushes have long been the standard for pastry brushes, but silicone brushes, which are relatively new on the market, make cleanup a snap. That said, I have found that egg wash applied to pastries with a natural-bristle brush goes on more evenly.

PIE PLATES AND TART PANS Before you start baking, check to make sure you have the right pan and the size called for in the recipe. Glass and stainless-steel pie pans are inexpensive, and nonstick-coated steel are even less expensive; I keep 9- and 10-inch pans on hand. The traditional aluminum tart pans with removable bottoms are the best for even browning. When ready to serve dessert, slip off the sides of the pan, slide the tart off the base onto a pedestal cake stand, and you have a buffet-ready presentation.

ROLLING PIN For pie and tart makers, high-quality tools make baking a pleasure. Invest in a heavy, thick pin at least 12 inches long, made of hardwood or marble. It's a tool for a lifetime. American-style rolling pins have handles, while French-style pins do not. Both work equally well; the type you choose is a matter of personal preference.

SPRINGFORM PAN Built with separate sides that clamp onto (and then unclamp from) the bottom, this pan is great for cheesecakes and other cakes that are difficult to unmold. Springform pans come in aluminum, stainless steel, or nonstick. I prefer the aluminum ones. For this book, you will need a 9- or 10-inch pan with 2-inch sides.

STAND MIXER I've had my KitchenAid stand mixer made by Hobart for almost thirty years.

It is sturdy, heavy, and dependable. I bought an extra mixing bowl and an extra whip attachment so I could swap out a used bowl or beater without needing to stop and wash the dirty one. This is especially helpful if you are making a cake that requires the yolks and whites to be beaten separately. The new KitchenAid mixers are manufactured in China and don't seem to be as dependable as the old ones, so it is worth looking at other brands. A good mixer should be a lifetime investment. That said, you can get by with a handheld mixer for all of the recipes in this book.

WIRE COOLING RACKS It's convenient to have 2 racks on hand, or enough to cool 2 dozen cookies. These don't need to be expensive; they do need to be sturdy.

OTHER HANDY TOOLS Other useful items to keep in mind when planning a menu or browsing cooking shops are a pie server, an offset spatula for icing cakes, a bread knife, heatproof silicone spatulas, a grater, a kitchen timer, ladles, and decorative cutters for pie making.

1

Appetizers

Today, Thanksgiving's sport du jour is football, a game that didn't become an integral part of American life until the early twentieth century. Celebrants at the first Thanksgiving, however, had ample opportunity to demonstrate their athletic prowess. They enjoyed shooting competitions with bows and arrows and muskets, lacrosse, foot races, and wrestling. Marathon eating, however, was and still is the main sporting event of the day, so let the games begin with Rogue River Blue Cheese Wafers with Celery Crudités, Wild Mushroom and Goat Cheese Puff Pastry Pockets, and Tex-Mex Honey Pecans.

Vermont Farmhouse Cheddar Cheese Straws

MAKES 30 CHEESE STRAWS

It's the spicy and sharp flavor of traditionally made farmhouse Cheddars that delivers the deep, rich taste of these crisp cheese straws. The small state of Vermont has a long history of making Cheddar cheese by the traditional methods of the English. Vermont cheese maker Cabot makes wonderful Cheddars; the Clothbound Cheddar is a personal favorite. In fact, this cheese, the joint effort of Cabot Creamery and Jasper Hill Farms, won the Best of Show award from the American Cheese Society in 2006.

This recipe doubles easily for 60 straws.

1 sheet **FROZEN PUFF PASTRY DOUGH** (from a 17.3-ounce package)

1 cup (4 ounces) shredded **SHARP CHEDDAR CHEESE**

1 tablespoon snipped **FRESH CHIVES**

1 teaspoon minced **FRESH THYME**

¾ teaspoon *PIMENTÓN* (Spanish smoked paprika)

¼ teaspoon **CAYENNE PEPPER**

ALL-PURPOSE FLOUR for dusting

1 **LARGE EGG**, beaten with 2 teaspoons water

Remove 1 pastry sheet from the package and let thaw at room temperature for 30 minutes. Tightly seal the remaining pastry and freeze for another use.

Position one rack in the center and a second rack in the lower third of the oven and preheat to 425°F. Have ready 2 rimmed baking sheets, preferably nonstick. For pans without a nonstick finish, line the pans with parchment paper or use Silpat mats.

In a small bowl, mix together the cheese, chives, thyme, *pimentón*, and cayenne pepper. Set aside.

Unfold the pastry sheet and place it on a lightly floured cutting board. If there are any cracks in the pastry, gently pinch them closed. Using a lightly floured rolling pin, roll over the pastry gently, just enough to remove the fold marks, and then roll it out into a 10-by-15-inch rectangle. Cut in half lengthwise to form two 5-by-15-inch rectangles. Brush each piece with the egg wash. Arrange 1 piece of the dough with the long side facing you and distribute the cheese filling evenly over it. Place the second piece of dough, egg wash side down, on top of the cheese, lining up the edges evenly. Using the rolling pin, press the sheets together to secure the cheese firmly between the layers, especially at the edges.

● ● CONTINUED ● ●

Using a sharp knife or pizza wheel, cut the filled and pressed pastry crosswise into 30 strips, each ½-inch wide. Working with 1 strip at a time, twist 3 times and lay the cheese straw on a baking sheet, pressing down the ends firmly to keep it from untwisting during baking. Continue to twist and arrange the remaining strips, placing them 1 inch apart on the baking sheets.

Bake for 8 minutes, switch the position of the baking sheets, and continue to bake until the cheese straws are puffed, golden brown, and crisp, about 4 to 6 minutes longer. Transfer to a wire rack and let cool slightly. Serve warm or at room temperature.

DO AHEAD   The cheese straws can be made up to 3 days in advance. Store in a lock-top plastic bag or an airtight container at room temperature. The day of serving, arrange the cheese straws on a rimmed baking sheet and crisp them for 7 to 10 minutes in a preheated 375°F oven.

Rogue River Blue Cheese Wafers with Celery Crudités

MAKES 35 WAFERS

European settlers brought celery to America in the 1600s, but the U.S. commercial celery industry did not take hold until the second half of the 1800s, when Dutch farmers in Michigan began marketing the crop. The industry spread to Florida and then west to California, where it is concentrated today. In the late 1800s, celery was considered a fancy new food worthy of celebrating; in season only from November through March, celery was expensive and served elegantly in its own footed celery glass. Today, celery is munched year-round as a low-calorie nibble, or stuffed with cream cheese or peanut butter as a favorite after-school snack. With the anticipation of an elaborate holiday meal ahead, delicate blue cheese topped puff pastry wafers served with celery crudités makes a light hors d'oeuvre. Make the cream cheese spread with award-winning blue cheese from Oregon, a regional favorite. Look to other regions for yet more stellar blue cheeses, such as Maytag Blue from Iowa or Point Reyes Blue from California.

Puff Pastry Wafers

1 sheet **FROZEN PUFF PASTRY DOUGH**, from a 17.3 ounce package

ALL-PURPOSE FLOUR for dusting

1 **LARGE EGG**, beaten

Blue Cheese Spread

1 cup (4 ounces) crumbled **BLUE CHEESE**

½ cup **CREAM CHEESE**, at room temperature

1 tablespoon finely snipped **FRESH CHIVES**

Remove one of the pastry sheets from the package and thaw the pastry at room temperature for 30 minutes. Tightly seal the remaining pastry and freeze for another use.

Position one oven rack in the center and preheat the oven to 425°F. Have ready two identically sized rimmed baking sheets and two sheets of parchment paper cut to fit the bottom of the pans.

Unfold the pastry sheet and place it on a lightly floured cutting board. Using a rolling pin, roll the pastry just enough to remove the fold marks. Using a 1¾-inch round cookie cutter, cut approximately 35 rounds of dough. Place the rounds on one of the parchment-lined baking sheets. Brush the tops of the pastry with beaten egg, being careful to not let the egg run down the sides. Cover with a sheet of parchment, and place the second (empty) baking sheet on top, so the

● ● CONTINUED ● ●

● ● CONTINUED ● ●

Freshly ground **PEPPER**

SWEET PAPRIKA, for garnish

8 to 10 ribs **CELERY**, tops left intact
and bottoms trimmed

baking sheets nest together. (This will keep the pastry even and prevent it from rising too much, thus creating crisp wafers.) Bake for 15 minutes until crisp and light golden brown. Remove the top baking sheet and piece of parchment and let the wafers cool on the pan.

In a medium bowl, thoroughly mix together the blue cheese and cream cheese. Stir in the chives and add a few grinds of pepper. Taste and adjust the seasoning. Fill a pastry bag with a medium open star pastry tip to form rosettes. Form rosettes of the blue cheese spread in the center of each puff pastry wafer. Garnish with a light dusting of paprika. Arrange on a serving tray.

To prepare the celery, trim the tops of the non-leafy celery ribs. Leave the tops on the tender inner ribs. Use a vegetable peeler to peel the strings from the back of the larger ribs. Cut the celery in half lengthwise and then cut crosswise into 3-inch-long strips. Arrange vertically in a decorative glass or narrow bowl.

Serve the blue cheese wafers and crudités immediately, or cover loosely with plastic wrap and refrigerate for up to 1 hour.

DO AHEAD   Make the puff pastry wafers up to 1 day in advance. Make the blue cheese spread up to 2 days in advance and store in an airtight container in the refrigerator. Remove from the refrigerator 1 hour before piping or spreading on the wafers. Prepare the celery up to 1 day in advance. Wrap the celery in a damp paper towel and store in a lock-top plastic bag in the refrigerator.

Crostini with Fig and Kalamata Olive Tapenade

MAKES 1½ CUPS

Welcome your Thanksgiving guests with a lusty appetizer, blending sweet and salty flavors in an easy, do-ahead tapenade. In this savory spread, the rich taste and intriguing texture of plumped dried figs contrasts with salt-brined purple-black olives, pine nuts, capers, and a hint of oregano. Blended with a dash of balsamic vinegar and deeply flavored extra-virgin olive oil, this tapenade is the perfect topper for crostini.

1½ cups finely chopped, dried **BLACK MISSION FIGS**, stems removed

½ cup **WATER**

½ cup **KALAMATA OLIVES**, pitted and chopped

⅓ cup **PINE NUTS**, toasted (see Cook's Note)

2 tablespoons **BALSAMIC VINEGAR**

2 tablespoons **EXTRA-VIRGIN OLIVE OIL**

2 tablespoons **SMALL CAPERS**, rinsed and blotted dry

1½ tablespoons chopped **FRESH OREGANO LEAVES**

½ teaspoon **KOSHER SALT**

½ teaspoon freshly ground **BLACK PEPPER**

Crostini (page 30)

Place the figs and water in a small saucepan and bring the water to a simmer over medium-low heat. Cook until the figs are softened and the liquid has evaporated, about 7 minutes. Transfer the figs to a medium bowl. Add the olives, pine nuts, vinegar, oil, capers, oregano, salt, and pepper. Mix gently to combine. Transfer to a serving bowl, cover, and set aside at room temperature for 1 hour to allow the flavors to meld. Serve with crostini.

COOK'S NOTE

Place a small, heavy skillet over medium-high heat. When it is hot, but not smoking, add the pine nuts. Stirring constantly, toast them for 3 to 5 minutes until nicely browned. Transfer to a plate and set aside to cool.

DO AHEAD

Make the tapenade up to 5 days in advance and store in an airtight container in the refrigerator. Remove from the refrigerator 1 hour before serving.

Crostini

Crostini means "little toasts" in Italian. They are small, thin slices of toasted bread, usually brushed with olive oil and baked. If you want plain toasts, simply omit the oil.

1 **BAGUETTE**, about 1½ inches in diameter

EXTRA-VIRGIN OLIVE OIL for brushing

Position one rack in the center and a second rack in the upper third of the oven and preheat to 350°F. Cut the baguette into slices ⅓ inch thick and arrange in a single layer on 2 baking sheets. Brush lightly on both sides with olive oil. Bake for about 7 minutes until lightly browned on top. Turn the slices and switch the position of the baking sheets. Bake for about 5 minutes longer until the crostini are lightly browned on the second side. They should be crunchy but not brittle. Serve warm or at room temperature.

DO AHEAD

The crostini can be made up to 3 days in advance. Store in a lock-top plastic bag or an airtight container at room temperature.

Deviled Eggs with Capers and Wild Smoked Salmon

MAKES 24 STUFFED EGGS

Northwest Native Americans pinned whole fillets of salmon to alder planks, built a large bonfire, and placed the planks upright, close to and around the fire in order to smoke-cook the salmon and preserve it. Pairing this lusciously smoked fish with the creamy filling of classic deviled eggs takes these from picnic fare to spectacular hors d'oeuvres—a terrific beginning to a Thanksgiving feast. Of course, if you want to make traditional deviled eggs, just skip the salmon in the recipe.

1 dozen large **EGGS** (see Cook's Note)

½ cup **MAYONNAISE**

2 tablespoons **FRESH LEMON JUICE**

6 ounces **ALDER-SMOKED WILD SALMON OR COLD-SMOKED SALMON** (lox), finely diced

2 tablespoons **PETITE CAPERS**, rinsed and drained

1 tablespoon minced **FRESH DILL**, plus 24 tiny sprigs for garnish (optional)

Freshly ground **PEPPER**

Place the eggs in a saucepan large enough to fit them without crowding and add cold water to cover by 1½ inches. Bring to a boil over medium-high heat, then reduce the heat to low and simmer the eggs for 10 minutes. Remove from the heat and run cold water over the eggs in the pan until cooled. When cool, working with 1 egg at a time, gently crack the shell all over and carefully peel under cool running water. Blot dry.

Cut the peeled eggs in half lengthwise and transfer the yolks to a small bowl. Arrange the egg white halves on a serving platter. Set aside while you make the filling.

Using a fork, mash the egg yolks to a smooth consistency. Using a rubber spatula, fold in the mayonnaise and lemon juice and blend to a smooth paste. Add the salmon, capers, dill, and a few grinds of pepper and mix until evenly distributed.

To assemble and serve, fit a pastry bag with a plain or large star tip. Fold back the top of the bag to form a collar. Use a rubber spatula to scrape the egg yolk filling into the bag. Twist the top of the bag and squeeze the filling down to the tip, squeezing out any air pockets. Hold the bag upright and pipe a rosette into each egg white half. (Alternatively, use a butter knife to mound the filling in the egg white halves.) Garnish each half with a tiny sprig of dill, if you like. Arrange on a platter and serve immediately.

•• CONTINUED ••

Deviled Eggs with Capers and Wild Smoked Salmon

COOK'S NOTE For hard-cooked eggs, it is better to use eggs that are 1 week to 10 days old rather than fresh eggs, as fresh eggs can be harder to peel. Deviled eggs look the best when the yolks are centered in the whites, so try one of these tricks for centering: Either cook the eggs standing up in an egg rack, or store the eggs on their sides for 12 to 24 hours before hard-cooking them. This is easily accomplished by securing the carton of eggs closed with tape or rubber bands and turning the carton on its side in the refrigerator.

DO AHEAD You can boil the eggs up to 4 days in advance and refrigerate them. You can peel and halve the eggs and make the filling up to 1 day in advance. Cover and refrigerate. Assemble the eggs, garnish, and arrange on a platter up to 4 hours before serving. Cover lightly with plastic wrap and refrigerate. Remove from the refrigerator just before serving.

Tex-Mex Honey Pecans

MAKES 2 CUPS PECANS

Native pecan trees now grow along almost every river in Texas, but this was not always true. Shortly before Texas Governor Hogg died in 1906, he requested that a pecan tree be planted at his grave, and the nuts be given out to the people of Texas to plant. He wanted Texas to become a land of trees. In 1919, the Texas state legislature voted to make the pecan the state tree. The peak season for pecans is during the autumn months, so buy fresh-from-the-orchard shelled pecans and roast them with this sweet-and-savory blend of spices and honey. Trust me, these disappear in a hurry, so you might want to double the recipe.

2 tablespoons **HONEY**

1 teaspoon **CHIPOTLE POWDER**

¼ teaspoon **GROUND CINNAMON**

¼ teaspoon **GROUND ALLSPICE**

2 cups (8 ounces) **PECAN HALVES**

2 tablespoons **SUGAR**

1 teaspoon **KOSHER OR COARSE SEA SALT**

Preheat the oven to 325°F. Have ready a rimmed baking sheet, preferably non-stick. For pans without a nonstick finish, line the pan with parchment paper or use a Silpat mat.

In a large nonstick skillet over medium heat, warm the honey to thin it, then stir in the chipotle powder, cinnamon, and allspice. Add the pecans and stir until evenly coated with the honey mixture.

Spread the nuts in a single layer on the baking sheet. Bake for about 10 minutes until aromatic, glistening, and lightly browned. Transfer the pan to a wire rack and let cool for 2 minutes.

In a medium bowl, combine the sugar and salt. Add the warm pecans and toss with the sugar and salt until evenly coated. Spread the pecans on a clean sheet of parchment or waxed paper and let cool to room temperature. Store in a lock-top plastic bag or an airtight container at room temperature.

DO AHEAD The nuts can be made up to 1 week in advance. If the nuts aren't as crisp as when first baked, refresh them in a 400°F oven for 3 to 5 minutes a few hours before serving them.

Wild Mushroom and Goat Cheese Puff Pastry Pockets

MAKES 48 POCKETS

In the fall, as the rains come, the ground dampens, and the leaves fall, the farmers' markets start brimming with wild mushrooms. I bring home a bagful, clean and chop them, and then sauté them in butter or olive oil. I first made this filling for omelets and decided it would be ideal for hors d'oeuvres. These puff pastry pockets are simple to make and freeze beautifully. Have them ready to pop in the oven throughout the holiday season.

2 sheets **FROZEN PUFF PASTRY DOUGH** (from a 17.3-ounce package)

Mushroom Filling

1 pound **ASSORTED WILD AND CULTI-VATED MUSHROOMS** such as cremini, shiitake, and chanterelle, wiped or brushed clean, stem ends trimmed

3 tablespoons **EXTRA-VIRGIN OLIVE OIL**

2 **SHALLOTS**, finely minced

1½ teaspoons **KOSHER OR SEA SALT**

Freshly ground **PEPPER**

2 tablespoons minced **FRESH FLAT-LEAF PARSLEY**

1 tablespoon minced **FRESH DILL**

1 teaspoon minced **FRESH THYME**

¼ cup (2 ounces) **FRESH GOAT CHEESE**, at room temperature

ALL-PURPOSE FLOUR for dusting

1 **LARGE EGG**, beaten with 2 teaspoons water

Remove the pastry sheets from the package and let thaw at room temperature for 30 minutes.

To make the mushroom filling, chop the mushrooms finely and set aside. In a large skillet over medium-high heat, warm the olive oil and swirl to coat the pan. Add the shallots and sauté for about 2 minutes until just beginning to soften. Add the mushrooms and sauté, stirring frequently, for about 3 minutes until they just begin to soften. Add the salt and a few grinds of pepper and continue to sauté for about 5 minutes longer until the mushrooms give off their juices. Add the parsley, dill, thyme, and goat cheese to the pan. Sauté, stirring constantly, for 2 to 3 minutes longer until most of the liquid has evaporated and the goat cheese is blended in. Remove from the heat. Set aside and let cool.

Position one rack in the center and a second rack in the lower third of the oven and preheat to 425°F. Have ready 2 rimmed baking sheets, preferably nonstick. For pans without a nonstick finish, line the pans with parchment paper or use Silpat mats.

Unfold 1 of the pastry sheets and place it on a lightly floured cutting board. If there are any cracks in the pastry, gently pinch them closed. Using a lightly floured rolling pin, roll over the pastry gently, just enough to remove the fold marks, and then roll it out into a 10-by-15-inch rectangle. Using a sharp knife or pizza wheel, cut the pastry sheet lengthwise into four 2½-by-15-inch strips. Cut each strip crosswise into 6 equal pieces to form a total of twenty-four 2½-inch squares. Repeat with the second sheet of pastry.

•• CONTINUED ••

Brush each square with the egg wash on the side facing up. Put a rounded teaspoon of filling in the center of each square. Gather the four corners and bring them up to the center, pinching the dough together firmly to secure it at the point, forming square pouches. Leave the seams along the edges open so some of the mushroom filling shows. Transfer the mushroom pockets to the baking sheets, placing them about 1 inch apart. Lightly dab the sides of the pockets with any remaining egg wash.

Bake for 10 minutes, switch the position of the baking sheets, and continue to bake for about 4 to 6 minutes longer until the pockets are puffed, golden brown on the sides and bottom, and crisp. Transfer to a wire rack and let cool slightly. Serve warm or at room temperature.

DO AHEAD   The mushroom filling can be cooled, covered, and refrigerated for up to 3 days. Remove the filling from the refrigerator 1 hour before filling the pastry pockets to soften it slightly. The mushroom pockets can be made and assembled completely and frozen, unbaked. Freeze the unbaked pastries on rimmed baking sheets, and then transfer them to a freezer container, arranging the pockets in layers between sheets of waxed paper. The pastries can be frozen for up to 1 month. Bake the pockets without thawing first; the baking times will be longer, about 20 to 25 minutes, so follow the recipe's doneness cues.

Warm Maryland Crab Dip with Lemon Panko Topping

SERVES 8

Marylanders love seafood from the Chesapeake Bay. The meat from the famous blue crabs of those waters is made into crab cakes, bisques, dips, and spreads. This dip highlights the crab flavor and texture without masking it and makes a light counterpoint to the Thanksgiving feast to follow. Make your own crostini, up to 3 days in advance, or simply buy crackers to serve with the dip.

1 tablespoon **UNSALTED BUTTER**

1 large **SHALLOT**, minced

½ cup (4 ounces) **CREAM CHEESE**, at room temperature

¼ cup **HEAVY (WHIPPING) CREAM**

3 tablespoons **MAYONNAISE**

1 tablespoon **DIJON MUSTARD**

1 tablespoon **FRESH LEMON JUICE**

⅓ cup thinly sliced **GREEN ONIONS**, including green tops

1½ tablespoons minced **FRESH FLAT-LEAF PARSLEY**

¾ teaspoon **KOSHER OR SEA SALT**

⅛ teaspoon **CAYENNE PEPPER**

1 pound **FRESH LUMP CRABMEAT**, picked over for shells and well drained

● ● CONTINUED ● ●

In a medium skillet, melt the butter over medium heat. Add the shallot and sauté for about 2 minutes until soft but not browned. Remove from the heat. Add the cream cheese, cream, mayonnaise, mustard, and lemon juice. Using a rubber spatula, stir to combine, then fold in the green onions, parsley, salt, and cayenne pepper. Fold in the crabmeat, breaking up any large chunks with a fork. Transfer the crab dip to a shallow baking dish. Set aside.

Position a rack in the upper third of the oven and preheat to 425°F.

● ● CONTINUED ● ●

Lemon Panko Topping

3 tablespoons **UNSALTED BUTTER**

⅔ cup **PANKO** (Japanese bread crumbs) or other unseasoned bread crumbs

1½ teaspoons freshly grated **LEMON ZEST**

Pinch of **KOSHER OR SEA SALT**

Crostini for serving (page 30)

To make the topping, in a small skillet, melt the butter over medium heat. Add the *panko* and toast, stirring constantly, for about 2 minutes until the crumbs are golden brown and crisp. Remove from the heat and stir in the lemon zest and salt. Scatter the topping evenly over the crab dip. Bake until heated through and bubbly at the edges and the topping is golden, 12 to 15 minutes. Serve warm with the crostini.

DO AHEAD   The crab dip, without the *panko* topping, can be prepared up to 1 day in advance. Cover and refrigerate. Remove from the refrigerator 1 hour before baking. The *panko* topping can be prepared up to 1 day in advance. Transfer to an airtight container and store at room temperature. Scatter the topping over the crab dip just before baking.

Crostini with Gulf Shrimp, Jalapeño, and Lime

MAKES 24 CROSTINI

These sweet-tasting Gulf shrimp are beautifully pink after gentle cooking in a citrus-and-spice-infused bath. Their delicate flavor is enrobed in a touch of cream cheese, with bright accents of jalapeño chile and green onion and a splash of fresh lime juice, just enough to bind them as a topping for crisp crostini.

½ **LEMON**, cut into thin slices

1 **BAY LEAF**

10 **PEPPERCORNS**

1¾ teaspoons **KOSHER OR SEA SALT**

1⅓ pounds medium (31–35 count) **UNCOOKED SHRIMP** in the shell

3 tablespoons minced **GREEN ONIONS**, including green tops

2 teaspoons minced **JALAPEÑO CHILE**, seeds and ribs removed (see Cook's Note)

2 teaspoons freshly grated **LIME ZEST**

2 tablespoons **FRESH LIME JUICE**

½ cup (3 ounces) **WHIPPED CREAM CHEESE**

Crostini (page 30)

1 **LIME**, halved lengthwise and thinly sliced

In a medium saucepan, combine the lemon slices, bay leaf, peppercorns, and salt. Add 5 cups of cold water and bring to a boil over high heat. Simmer for 10 minutes. Reduce the heat to medium-low and add the shrimp. Cook for about 3 minutes just until the shrimp are pink and cooked through. Drain in a colander and rinse under cold water. Peel and devein the shrimp. Discard the lemon slices and spices. Cut 12 of the shrimp in half lengthwise and set aside for garnish. Finely chop the remaining shrimp and transfer to a medium bowl.

Add the green onions, chile, lime zest and juice, and cream cheese to the bowl with the shrimp. Stir until the ingredients are well combined. Taste and adjust the seasoning.

To assemble and serve, mound a spoonful of the shrimp mixture on each crostini. Garnish each crostini with a reserved shrimp half and thin slice of lime. Arrange on a serving platter and serve immediately, or cover lightly with plastic wrap and set aside at room temperature for up to 30 minutes.

COOK'S NOTE

Keep some disposable surgical gloves on hand (available at any pharmacy) to wear while working with fresh chiles. They will keep the capsaicin, the caustic compound that is naturally present in chiles, from irritating your skin.

DO AHEAD

The shrimp mixture along with the shrimp reserved for the garnish can be prepared up to 1 day in advance. Cover tightly and refrigerate.

2

Soups and Salads

The cornucopia, also referred to as the horn of plenty or harvest cone, is one of Thanksgiving's most recognizable symbols. It resembles a goat's horn and dates back more than 2,500 years to the ancient Greeks and the horn possessed by Zeus's nurse. The first course at Thanksgiving dinner can be a marvelous opportunity to serve up a cornucopia-style array of harvest foods in brilliant soups and salads—a plan that is also practical, as it gives the busy cook more time to choreograph the rest of the meal. Use the fantastic bounty of the season to make splendid starters like Roasted Chestnut Soup with Pumpernickel Croutons; Spinach Salad with Bosc Pears, Cranberries, Red Onion, and Toasted Hazelnuts; and Butter Lettuce Salad with Persimmons and Pomegranates.

Butternut Squash Bisque with a Fried Sage and Popcorn Garnish

SERVES 6

This bisque is deeply rich and full flavored because the squash and apples are roasted first, which allows the natural sugars to caramelize. It's an easy method with spectacular results, and the popcorn with fried sage leaves makes a tasty and whimsical garnish. Making this soup 3 days in advance feels like a real jump start to a busy cooking schedule. Serve the bisque as a first course at the table or, as a casual alternative, ladle it into mugs for sipping before dinner.

2 pounds **BUTTERNUT SQUASH**, peeled, halved lengthwise, seeded, and cut into 2-inch chunks

2 tablespoons **EXTRA-VIRGIN OLIVE OIL**

2 **GRANNY SMITH APPLES** (about 1 pound total weight), halved lengthwise and cored

4 cups **HOMEMADE CHICKEN STOCK** (see page 11) **OR CANNED LOW-SODIUM CHICKEN BROTH**

½ cup **HEAVY (WHIPPING) CREAM**

¼ teaspoon freshly grated **NUTMEG**

1 tablespoon **SUGAR**

KOSHER OR SEA SALT

Freshly ground **PEPPER**

Garnish

¾ cup **CANOLA OIL**

⅓ cup **FRESH SAGE LEAVES**

KOSHER SALT

1 mini bag (1.5 ounces) **MICROWAVE POPCORN**

Preheat the oven to 350°F.

In a large bowl, toss the squash with the olive oil. Spread in a single layer on a large rimmed baking sheet. Place the apples, cut side down, on the baking sheet. Roast for about 30 to 35 minutes until the squash and apples are tender when pierced with a fork.

Place the roasted squash in a food processor fitted with the metal blade. Use a spoon to scrape the flesh of the apples into the food processor and discard the skins. Process the squash and apples to a smooth purée. Add 1 cup of the stock and continue processing until smooth. Transfer the squash mixture to a medium saucepan and add the remaining 3 cups stock, the cream, nutmeg, and sugar. Bring to a boil, then reduce the heat to maintain a simmer and cook for 10 minutes. Season to taste with salt and pepper. Set aside and keep warm.

To make the garnish, in a heavy 8-inch sauté pan, heat the canola oil until it registers 365°F on a deep-frying thermometer. It should be hot, but not smoking. Have ready a small baking sheet lined with a double thickness of paper towels. Working quickly, fry half of the sage leaves for about 5 seconds and, using a slotted spoon, transfer to the paper towels. Fry the remaining sage leaves in the same way. Generously sprinkle the sage leaves with kosher salt and set aside. (Reserve the cooking oil for another use, such as sautéing vegetables or potatoes; it will be delicately flavored with sage.)

●● CONTINUED ●●

CONTINUED Butternut Squash Bisque with a Fried Sage and
Popcorn Garnish

To make the popcorn garnish, microwave the popcorn according to the package directions. Transfer to a bowl and sprinkle with salt, if needed. (A mini bag of popcorn makes about 4 cups popped corn. You'll need a generous cupful for the garnish for this soup; snack on the rest.)

To serve, ladle the soup into warmed individual bowls and garnish with the fried sage leaves and popcorn. Serve hot.

DO AHEAD The soup can be made up to 3 days in advance. Let cool completely and refrigerate in a covered container. Rewarm gently just before serving. The sage leaves can be fried and kept at room temperature up to 4 hours in advance.

Silky Parsnip-Potato Soup with Crisp Diced Bacon

SERVES 8

The parsnip, a root vegetable related to the carrot, was brought to America in the early 1600s. Underappreciated in the vegetable family, this creamy-white root can be boiled, sautéed, roasted, and steamed. At their peak during the fall and winter, parsnips' naturally sweet flavor develops when the first frost converts the starches to sugar. Deeply flavored and aromatic, this soup is perfect winter comfort food.

4 tablespoons **UNSALTED BUTTER**

1 large **YELLOW ONION**, chopped (about 2 cups)

1½ pounds **PARSNIPS**, peeled and cut into 1-inch chunks

1 pound **RUSSET POTATOES**, peeled and cut into 1-inch chunks

¼ cup **DRY SHERRY** (fino)

6 cups **HOMEMADE CHICKEN STOCK** (see page 11) **OR CANNED LOW-SODIUM CHICKEN BROTH**

3 sprigs **FRESH THYME**

3 sprigs **FRESH FLAT-LEAF PARSLEY**

2 **BAY LEAVES**

1 cup **HEAVY (WHIPPING) CREAM**

KOSHER OR SEA SALT

Freshly ground **WHITE PEPPER**

5 strips **BACON**, cut into ½-inch dice

In a stockpot, melt the butter over medium-low heat. Add the onion. Cover and cook, stirring occasionally, for about 8 minutes until the onion is soft but not browned. Add the parsnips and potatoes and cook for about 2 minutes, stirring constantly, until well coated with the butter. Add the sherry and raise the heat to medium-high. Sauté the vegetables, stirring constantly, until most of the liquid has evaporated, about 1 minute. Add the stock. Place the thyme, parsley, and bay leaves in a square of cheesecloth and tie with kitchen twine to make a bouquet garni. Add to the pot and bring to a boil. Reduce the heat to maintain a simmer, cover partially, and cook for about 30 minutes until the vegetables are tender and soft enough to purée.

Let the soup cool for about 10 minutes. Discard the bouquet garni. Working in batches, process the soup to a smooth purée in a blender or food processor fitted with the metal blade. Return the puréed soup to the pot and add the cream. Cook over low heat until heated through, but do not let the soup boil. Season to taste with salt and pepper. Set aside and keep warm.

In a skillet, cook the bacon over medium heat for about 5 minutes until crisp. Transfer to a plate lined with paper towels to drain.

Ladle the soup into a warmed tureen or individual bowls, garnish with the bacon.

DO AHEAD

The soup can be made up to 3 days in advance. Cool completely and refrigerate in a covered container. Rewarm gently just before serving. The bacon can be cooked up to 1 day in advance and stored, covered, in the refrigerator. Crisp in a skillet or on medium power in a microwave.

Oyster Stew

SERVES 6

Oysters, along with clams and lobsters, have been harvested and relished by Native Americans along the Atlantic coast from very early times. When the English colonists arrived on the shores of North America, they recognized the richness of the sea in the abundance of the excellent, large oysters. It is thought that the Native Americans taught the settlers how to tong or secure the bivalves with leather, and to dry them for winter food. Oysters were the most popular seafood along the Eastern seaboard during the nineteenth century, with oyster saloons serving raw and roasted oysters. Timeworn cookbooks have recipes for oyster stew, oyster soup, oyster pie, and oyster stuffing. For oyster lovers like me, this stew is irresistible.

1 pint (about 30) extra-small **SHUCKED OYSTERS** in their liquor (see page 13)

4 tablespoons **UNSALTED BUTTER**

1 tablespoon **WORCESTERSHIRE SAUCE**

1½ teaspoons **SWEET PAPRIKA**

½ teaspoon **CELERY SALT**

2 cups **WHOLE MILK**

1 cup **HEAVY (WHIPPING) CREAM**

¼ teaspoon freshly grated **NUTMEG**

KOSHER OR SEA SALT

Freshly ground **WHITE PEPPER**

2 tablespoons minced **FRESH FLAT-LEAF PARSLEY**

Drain the oysters through a fine-mesh sieve placed over a small bowl to catch the oyster liquor. Set the oysters aside. Reserve the liquor.

In a medium saucepan, melt the butter over medium heat. Stir in the Worcestershire sauce, paprika, and celery salt. Add the oysters and bring to a simmer. Cook just until the edges of the oysters curl. Add the oyster liquor to the pan and return to a simmer. Add the milk, cream, and nutmeg. Reduce the heat to low and cook, stirring occasionally, until heated through, but do not let the soup boil. Season to taste with salt and pepper.

Ladle the soup into a warmed tureen or individual bowls, garnish with the parsley, and serve hot.

DO AHEAD

Although it can be gently reheated successfully, oyster stew is best when made right before serving. Have everything measured and ready to cook—the soup is super simple to put together.

Creamy Mushroom Soup with Parmesan-and-Herb Croutons

SERVES 8   Portobellos, the oversized, dark, densely textured mushrooms in the produce aisle, are the perfect base for cold-weather soups. They have a meaty, rich taste that makes this soup intensely flavored without adding a long list of ingredients. Garnishing the puréed soup with Parmesan-and-herb-coated croutons adds a tangy, salty, crunchy finish—for a spectacular start to the Thanksgiving meal.

4 tablespoons **UNSALTED BUTTER**

2 **LEEKS**, white and light green parts only, halved lengthwise and thinly sliced

1 large **YELLOW ONION**, chopped

3 large **PORTOBELLO MUSHROOMS** (about 1 pound total weight), wiped or brushed clean and chopped

3 tablespoons **ALL-PURPOSE FLOUR**

6 cups **HOMEMADE CHICKEN STOCK** (see page 11) **OR CANNED LOW-SODIUM CHICKEN BROTH**

1½ tablespoons **FRESH THYME LEAVES**

1 **BAY LEAF**

1 teaspoon **KOSHER OR SEA SALT**

1 teaspoon **SUGAR**

½ teaspoon freshly ground **PEPPER**

1 cup **HEAVY (WHIPPING) CREAM**

● ● CONTINUED ● ●

In a stockpot, melt the butter over medium heat. Swirl to coat the bottom of the pot and add the leeks and onions. Cook, stirring constantly, for about 2 minutes until slightly softened and well coated with butter. Reduce the heat to very low, cover, and cook, stirring occasionally, for about 30 minutes until the leeks and onions are meltingly soft but not browned. Add the mushrooms and stir to combine. Cover and cook for 10 minutes. Raise the heat to medium, stir in the flour, and cook for 3 minutes. Add the stock, thyme, bay leaf, salt, sugar, and pepper. Bring to a simmer, cover partially, and cook for 10 minutes longer.

Let the soup cool for about 10 minutes. Discard the bay leaf. Working in batches, process the soup to a smooth purée in a blender or food processor fitted with the metal blade. Return the puréed soup to the pot and add the cream. Cook over low heat until heated through, but do not let the soup boil. Taste and adjust the seasoning. Keep the soup warm while you make the croutons. (Alternatively, the croutons can be made while the leeks and onion are cooking.)

● ● CONTINUED ● ●

Parmesan-and-Herb Croutons

5 cups **FRESH BREAD CUBES** (¾-inch cubes), cut from a loaf of artisan white bread with the crusts removed

¼ cup **EXTRA-VIRGIN OLIVE OIL**

½ cup (2 ounces) freshly grated **PARMESAN CHEESE**

¼ teaspoon freshly ground **PEPPER**

1 tablespoon minced **FRESH THYME**

½ tablespoon minced **FRESH OREGANO**

To make the croutons, preheat the oven to 375°F. In a large bowl, combine the bread cubes with the olive oil, cheese, and pepper and toss to coat evenly. Transfer to a rimmed baking sheet and bake for 6 minutes. Sprinkle the herbs over the bread cubes, toss to combine, and continue to bake until the bread cubes are crisp and golden, about 6 minutes longer.

Ladle the soup into warmed individual bowls, garnish with the croutons, and serve hot.

DO AHEAD   The soup can be made up to 3 days in advance. Let cool and refrigerate in a covered container. Rewarm gently just before serving. The croutons can be made up to 2 days in advance. Store in a lock-top plastic bag or airtight container at room temperature.

Roasted Chestnut Soup with Pumpernickel Croutons

SERVES 12

Nuts were an important source of protein and oil in the Native American diet. Along with acorns and walnuts, the Indians dried and stored chestnuts to enhance the food value of corn, considered a nutritionally poor staple. Historically, chestnuts—which contain twice as much starch as potatoes—were also ground into meal or flour for baked goods and puréed for puddings.

The American chestnut tree once covered almost nine million acres of eastern woodlands, from southern Ontario to northern Florida, but a fungus—it is thought unintentionally introduced into America from Asian chestnut trees that were imported as nursery stock—began killing this native species in the early 1900s and spread like wild-fire. Within forty years, most of the American chestnut trees in the eastern United States were completely destroyed. Today, most of the chestnut food crop is imported from Japan, China, Spain, and Italy, but chestnuts still figure as prominently in Thanksgiving recipes, from soups to stuffings, as they did centuries ago. If you have never peeled and eaten a freshly roasted chestnut, nor savored its aroma, you're in for a very special winter treat. Roast some and eat them out of hand—but also make this soup.

2 pounds **FRESH CHESTNUTS** (see Cook's Note and Do Ahead)

2 large **YELLOW ONIONS** (about 12 ounces each), cut into wedges about ½ inch thick

3 large **CARROTS**, peeled and cut into 1-inch chunks

3 tablespoons **EXTRA-VIRGIN OLIVE OIL**

•• CONTINUED ••

Position one rack in the center and a second rack in the lower third of the oven and preheat to 375°F. Using a sharp paring knife, make a long slash on the flat side of each chestnut, cutting through the outer shell and inner brown skin. Spread the chestnuts in a single layer on a rimmed baking sheet and roast for about 1 hour until tender when pierced with a fork. Every 15 minutes, sprinkle the chestnuts with a little water.

While the chestnuts are roasting, place the onions and carrots in a 9-by-13-inch baking pan. Drizzle with the olive oil and toss to coat thoroughly. Roast until tender when pierced with a fork, about 1 hour. Let the vegetables cool while you peel the chestnuts.

•• CONTINUED ••

8 cups **HOMEMADE CHICKEN STOCK** (see page 11) **OR CANNED LOW-SODIUM CHICKEN BROTH**

1 teaspoon **KOSHER OR SEA SALT**

Freshly ground **PEPPER**

1 cup **HEAVY (WHIPPING) CREAM**

Pumpernickel Croutons

3 tablespoons **EXTRA-VIRGIN OLIVE OIL**

5 slices **PUMPERNICKEL BREAD**, crusts removed, cut into ½-inch dice

Peel the chestnuts while they are still quite warm but cool enough to handle. Using the paring knife, remove the outer shells and the inner brown skins. Discard any chestnuts that look rotten. Set aside any chestnuts that are hard to peel, then rewarm them in the 400°F oven or place them on a paper towel and microwave on high for 45 seconds. Repeat as needed until easy to peel. You should have about 2½ cups peeled nuts.

In a medium bowl, combine the chestnuts and roasted vegetables and toss to mix. Place one-fourth of the mixture in a blender or food processor fitted with the metal blade. Add 2 cups of the stock and process to a uniformly coarse purée. (Do not overprocess to a smooth consistency; you want some texture for this soup.) Pour into a large saucepan. Repeat 3 times with the remaining chestnut mixture and stock. Add the salt and a few grinds of pepper. Bring to a boil over medium-high heat, then reduce the heat to maintain a gentle simmer and cook for about 20 minutes to allow the flavors to meld. Add the cream, stir to combine, and remove from the heat. Taste and adjust the seasoning. Keep the soup warm while you make the croutons. (Alternatively, make the croutons while the soup is simmering.)

To make the croutons, in a 12-inch sauté pan over medium-high heat, heat the olive oil and swirl to coat the pan. Add the bread cubes and gently stir until crisp on all sides, about 4 minutes. Using a slotted spoon, transfer the croutons to a plate lined with paper towels to drain.

Ladle the soup into warmed individual bowls, mound a spoonful of the croutons in the center of each, and serve hot.

COOK'S NOTE   If you prefer not to roast your own chestnuts, you can buy peeled chestnuts in vacuum-sealed packages, cans, or jars at specialty-food stores. You will need about 2½ cups. Drain any liquid in which they are packed. Prepared chestnuts are usually boiled rather than roasted, resulting in a bit of flavor loss. However, placing them on a rimmed baking sheet and roasting them in a 375°F oven for 15 minutes really improves their flavor. There is no question that using prepared chestnuts is a timesaving step.

DO AHEAD   Although peeling 2 pounds of chestnuts may seem tedious, it can be done up to 2 weeks in advance of making the soup. The roasted, peeled chestnuts can be frozen in lock-top freezer bags and then thawed at room temperature for 1 hour before using.

The soup can be made up to 3 days in advance. Let cool and refrigerate in a covered container. Rewarm gently just before serving. The croutons can be made up to 1 week ahead. Store in a lock-top plastic bag or an airtight container at room temperature.

Hearts of Romaine with Crisp Red Apples, Celery, and Cider Vinaigrette

SERVES 8

Thinking through all the soft foods on the Thanksgiving menu—sweet potatoes, mashed potatoes, stuffing, even cranberry sauce—I wanted to add a salad with crunch and style. The leaves from the hearts of romaine are left whole and arranged on a large platter like overlapping canoes. The apples and celery are marinated in the apple cider–sweetened dressing and then scattered over the dressed greens. This salad could be served as a light first course, set on a buffet with separate salad plates, or preset on the dinner table to accompany the main course.

Dressing

½ cup **EXTRA-VIRGIN OLIVE OIL**

3 tablespoons thawed **FROZEN APPLE JUICE CONCENTRATE**

2 tablespoons **APPLE CIDER VINEGAR**

¾ teaspoon **KOSHER OR SEA SALT**

½ teaspoon **SUGAR**

½ teaspoon freshly ground **PEPPER**

⅛ teaspoon **GROUND ALLSPICE**

2 **CRISP RED APPLES** such as Gala or Braeburn, halved, cored, and cut into paper-thin wedges

2 ribs **CELERY**, trimmed and cut on the diagonal into thin slices

4 **HEARTS OF ROMAINE**, halved lengthwise, leaves separated

Coarsely cracked **PEPPER**

To make the dressing, in a small jar with a tight-fitting lid, combine the olive oil, apple juice concentrate, vinegar, salt, sugar, pepper, and allspice. Cover tightly and shake vigorously to blend. Taste and adjust the seasoning. Set aside.

In a bowl, toss the apples and celery with 3 tablespoons of the dressing and let stand at room temperature to allow the flavors to meld, for at least 30 minutes or up to 1 hour.

To assemble the salad, place the romaine leaves in a large bowl. Give the remaining dressing a last-minute shake and pour over the greens. Toss to coat evenly. Arrange the leaves on a large serving platter or divide them evenly among 8 salad plates. Scatter the apples and celery over the top(s). Sprinkle with the coarsely cracked pepper and serve immediately.

DO AHEAD

The dressing can be made up to 1 day in advance, covered tightly, and refrigerated. Remove from the refrigerator 2 hours before serving.

Spinach Salad with Bosc Pears, Cranberries, Red Onion, and Toasted Hazelnuts

SERVES 8

This spinach salad speaks to all the wonderful autumnal flavors of the Pacific Northwest. The new crop of bronzed Bosc pears is piled high at the farmers' market; the hazelnuts have been harvested, shelled, and bagged for sale; and the cranberries arrive from the Long Beach, Washington, coastal bogs. I buy sweetened dried cranberries from a local producer, but they are readily available at the grocery store (Ocean Spray is a good-quality packager), found alongside raisins and other dried fruits. This salad is a snap to assemble if you buy the packaged prewashed and trimmed baby spinach.

Dressing

½ cup **EXTRA-VIRGIN OLIVE OIL**

2 tablespoons **BALSAMIC VINEGAR**

2 teaspoons **WHOLE-GRAIN MUSTARD**

1 teaspoon **SUGAR**

1 teaspoon **KOSHER OR SEA SALT**

Freshly ground **PEPPER**

1 cup thinly sliced **RED ONION**

⅓ cup **SWEETENED DRIED CRANBERRIES**

8 cups lightly packed **FRESH BABY SPINACH LEAVES**, stemmed if needed

2 firm but ripe **BOSC PEARS** (do not peel), quartered lengthwise, cored, and cut into long, thin slices

⅔ cup **HAZELNUTS**, toasted (see Cook's Notes) and chopped

To make the dressing, in a small jar with a tight-fitting lid, combine the olive oil, vinegar, mustard, sugar, salt, and pepper to taste. Cover tightly and shake vigorously to blend. Taste and adjust the seasoning. Set aside.

Place the onion in a medium bowl and cover with cold water. Let stand for 30 minutes. This crisps the onion and takes away the raw onion taste. Drain well and pat dry on paper towels.

In a small bowl, toss the cranberries with 2 tablespoons of the dressing to soften them. Set aside for at least 20 minutes or until ready to serve the salad.

To assemble the salad, place the spinach, onion, and pears in a large bowl. Give the remaining dressing a last-minute shake and pour over the salad. Toss to coat evenly. Arrange the salad in a large serving bowl or divide it evenly among 8 salad plates. Scatter the cranberries and hazelnuts over the top(s). Serve immediately.

●● CONTINUED ●●

CONTINUED Spinach Salad with Bosc Pears, Cranberries, Red Onion, and Toasted Hazelnuts

COOK'S NOTES   Try to buy shelled hazelnuts (also called filberts) with the brown, papery skins removed as well. To toast, spread the hazelnuts in a single layer on a rimmed baking sheet and place in a preheated 375°F oven. Toast for about 12 minutes until lightly browned. If the nuts still have the skins on, transfer them while they're hot to a clean kitchen towel. (Use a clean towel that is old or you don't mind washing with bleach, because the skins tend to discolor the fabric.) Rub the nuts to remove most of the skins (they never completely come off).

You can substitute unsalted cashews for the hazelnuts. Toast cashews, as directed above for hazelnuts, for 8 to 10 minutes until lightly browned.

DO AHEAD   The dressing can be made up to 1 day in advance, covered tightly, and refrigerated. Remove from the refrigerator 2 hours before serving. The nuts can be toasted up to 1 day in advance; store at room temperature in an airtight container. The onions and cranberries can be prepared up to 4 hours in advance. Set aside at room temperature.

Butter Lettuce Salad with Persimmons and Pomegranate

SERVES 10

For me, persimmons and pomegranates are two treasured fruits of winter. There is only a short gap between the luscious September tomatoes I love to add to salads and the crisp, sweetly acidic persimmons I use as their cold-weather substitute. Use the squat, tomato-shaped Fuyu persimmon for this salad. The skins should be orange-red, smooth, and shiny, and the flesh should feel firm to the touch, but not rock hard. The Hachiya persimmon, with pointy-tipped bottom is not the right variety of persimmon for salads.

Dressing

½ cup **EXTRA-VIRGIN OLIVE OIL**

⅓ cup **FRESH ORANGE JUICE** (from about 1 orange)

1 tablespoon **FRESH LEMON JUICE**

2 teaspoons **SUGAR**

¾ teaspoon **KOSHER OR SEA SALT**

Freshly ground **PEPPER**

2 tablespoons snipped **FRESH CHIVES**

2 tablespoons minced **FRESH FLAT-LEAF PARSLEY**

12 cups whole **BUTTER LETTUCE LEAVES** (about 3 heads; see Cook's Notes)

1 medium unblemished, firm and shiny **POMEGRANATE**

3 ripe **FUYU PERSIMMONS**, cored, halved, and cut into ¼-inch wedges

To make the dressing, in a small jar with a tight-fitting lid, combine the olive oil, orange juice, lemon juice, sugar, salt, and pepper to taste. Add the chives and parsley. Cover tightly and shake vigorously to blend. Taste and adjust the seasoning. Set aside.

Rinse the lettuce leaves and dry them in a salad spinner or pat dry with paper towels. Place the lettuce in a large bowl, cover with a slightly damp kitchen towel, and set aside until ready to serve.

To extract the seeds from the pomegranate, I suggest you wear an apron and disposable surgical gloves because the juice stains both hands and clothing. To remove the seeds, place a bowl of cool water in the sink. Cut off the crown of the pomegranate with a stainless-steel knife (a carbon-steel knife can turn the juice bitter) and scoop out some of the center membrane, or pith, with a spoon. Use the knife to score the skin into quarters, and then cut through enough of the membrane to see the seeds. Submerge the pomegranate in the water and break apart the quarters with your thumbs. Use your fingers to peel away the white membrane and pop out the seeds. The seeds will sink to the bottom of the bowl and the membrane will float to the top. Discard the membrane. Drain the seeds and spread them on a double thickness of paper towels to absorb the excess moisture. Set aside until ready to use.

● ● CONTINUED ● ●

To assemble the salad, add the persimmon wedges to the bowl of lettuce. Give the dressing a last-minute shake, pour over the salad, and toss well. Divide among individual salad plates and garnish each salad with as many pomegranate seeds as desired. (Save any remaining pomegranate seeds for another use.) Serve immediately.

COOK'S NOTES   I like to keep the butter lettuce leaves whole for an attractive presentation. You certainly can tear them into bite-sized pieces if you prefer. If butter lettuce is unavailable, use green or red leaf lettuce or a mixture of the two. In any case, be sure the lettuce is dried well; the dressing does not adhere to wet lettuce.

DO AHEAD   The dressing can be made up to 1 day in advance, covered tightly, and refrigerated. Remove from the refrigerator 2 hours before serving. The pomegranate can be prepared up to 1 day in advance. Place in a covered container and refrigerate. Remove from the refrigerator 2 hours before serving.

Chicory, Pear, and Toasted Pecan Salad with Buttermilk–Black Pepper Dressing

SERVES 8

If you are like me and adore bitter greens, then I urge you to make this delicious mix. I had never quite put together this flavor combination in a salad but was inspired to do so because I wanted to incorporate classic Southern ingredients. The buttermilk–black pepper dressing slicks the greens with a luscious coating of tang and spice. The toasted pecans add crunch, and the sliced Bosc pears lend sweetness. This is a wintertime favorite for my family.

Dressing

6 tablespoons **EXTRA-VIRGIN OLIVE OIL**

3 tablespoons **BUTTERMILK**

2 tablespoons **RICE VINEGAR**

1 tablespoon **MAYONNAISE**

½ teaspoon **KOSHER OR SEA SALT**

½ teaspoon **SUGAR**

¾ teaspoon freshly ground **PEPPER**

8 cups firmly packed **CHICORY** (curly endive), torn into bite-sized pieces

2 firm but ripe **BOSC PEARS** (do not peel), quartered lengthwise, cored, and cut into long, thin slices

½ cup coarsely chopped **TOASTED PECANS** (see Cook's Note)

To make the dressing, in a small jar with a tight-fitting lid, combine the olive oil, buttermilk, vinegar, mayonnaise, salt, sugar, and pepper. Cover tightly and shake vigorously to blend. Taste and adjust the seasoning. Set aside. The dressing can be made up to 1 day in advance, tightly covered, and refrigerated. Remove from the refrigerator 2 hours before serving.

To assemble the salad, place the chicory and pears in a large bowl. Give the dressing a last-minute shake and pour over the salad. Toss to coat evenly. Arrange the salad in a large serving bowl or divide it evenly among 8 salad plates. Scatter the pecans over the top(s). Serve immediately.

COOK'S NOTE

Toasting nuts brings out their full, rich flavor. Spread the pecans in a single layer on a rimmed baking sheet. Place in a preheated 350°F oven and toast for 7 to 10 minutes until lightly browned. Alternatively, the nuts can be toasted in a microwave oven. Spread in a single layer on a microwave-safe plate and microwave on high for about 2 to 3 minutes until lightly browned. The pecans can be toasted up to 1 day in advance. Store covered at room temperature.

Cabbage-and-Carrot Coleslaw with Lemon Mayonnaise

SERVES 10 TO 12

This recipe comes from my literary agent, Lisa Ekus-Saffer. A perennial joint effort of her mom and dad's, it is a must on their family Thanksgiving table. Jerry cuts the cabbage and grates the carrots; Diane makes the dressing. Like many wonderful cooks, they never measure a single ingredient. The amounts listed here will give you an incredible slaw, but do not be afraid to add a pinch more of this and a dash more of that. This is truly a recipe "to your taste" and improves overnight as the dressing saturates the cabbage.

1 head **GREEN CABBAGE** (about 3 pounds), quartered lengthwise and cored

3 large **CARROTS**, peeled

¾ cup **MAYONNAISE**

⅓ cup **FRESH LEMON JUICE**

2 teaspoons **SUGAR**

1 teaspoon **KOSHER OR SEA SALT**

½ teaspoon freshly ground **PEPPER**

¼ teaspoon **PAPRIKA**

Using a sharp knife, box grater, or food processor, thinly shred the cabbage. You should end up with about 6 lightly packed cups. Place the shredded cabbage in a large bowl. Using a box grater or food processor, thinly shred the carrots. You should have about 1½ cups. Add to the bowl with the cabbage and set aside.

In a small bowl, whisk together the mayonnaise, lemon juice, sugar, salt, pepper, and paprika. Add the dressing to the cabbage and carrots, stirring well to combine. Refrigerate for at least 1 hour, or preferably overnight, before serving.

3

Main Courses

Benjamin Franklin, in a puckish letter to his daughter, expressed displeasure that the bald eagle was chosen to symbolize America; he thought the turkey much more deserving of that honor. On Thanksgiving, at least, turkey *is* the national bird. Wild turkeys were numerous at the time of Plimoth Plantation, and the turkey we know and love was most likely on the earliest Thanksgiving table—although the Pilgrims used "turkey" more universally to mean any kind of wild fowl. Delight your company with such modern-day, regional classics as Spatchcocked Turkey Roasted with Lemon, Sage, and Garlic and Roast Turkey with Vidalia Cream Gravy. In addition to all the showcase turkeys in this chapter, I have included a Jack Daniel's Whiskey and Brown Sugar Crusted Ham for those who like to serve both ham and turkey for their feast. And for the vegetarians at your table, make them feel special with Molly's Pumpkin-and-Sage Lasagna, a spectacular meatless main course.

Buying a Turkey

The Choices

At one time, fresh or frozen was the only choice you had to make when it came to buying a commercially raised whole turkey. Now there are lots of choices, and quality and taste differences figure into them. Here are my thoughts on what is available in the marketplace.

STANDARD TURKEYS These mass-produced, conventionally raised birds are sold either fresh or frozen during the holiday season. This is a perfectly acceptable turkey, easy to obtain without a lot of forethought from any large supermarket, and reasonably priced.

SELF-BASTING TURKEYS These turkeys, sold fresh or frozen, have been "enhanced" with fat of some sort, in addition to natural and artificial flavorings. The selling point of this product is that the bird doesn't need to be basted, thus saving the cook time and energy. Good idea in theory, bad idea in practice—primarily because that enhancer is flavored vegetable oil, which is not a likely source for any improvement, in my opinion. This is my least favorite turkey on the market. Do not brine a self-basting turkey; these birds have already been injected with a salt solution.

FREE-RANGE TURKEYS These are the turkeys that get to run around the barnyard, so to speak. They aren't necessarily ranging outdoors, but they are raised in spacious, open environments.

Most of these birds are more expensive than other turkeys, especially if they are also organic, which free-range turkeys often are. If you order from a knowledgeable butcher or have a specialty-foods store you trust, ask the staff who farms the turkeys they sell and if the birds are both free range and organic, or "natural" and free range, which means they are not fed organic feed but are raised without hormones or antibiotics. These can be delicious, moist, and flavorful birds, and I believe they are usually worth the higher price.

KOSHER TURKEYS Although usually sold frozen, kosher birds are often available fresh in large supermarkets at Thanksgiving. They have been inspected, slaughtered, and cleaned under strict rabbinical supervision, which makes for an expensive bird. If you will be serving observant Jewish guests, this is the turkey to buy; otherwise, opt for a nonkosher, free-range bird. Do not brine kosher turkeys, as they have already been salted in the koshering process.

HERITAGE TURKEYS Prized for their rich flavor and beautiful plumage, Bourbon Red, American Bronze, Slate, and Narragansett are four breeds of turkey that date all the way back to the Pilgrims. These breeds reproduce naturally (unlike the broad-breasted breed of turkey that requires artificial insemination to reproduce) and tend to be raised by small specialty producers who allow the turkeys to range freely in large, field-fenced pastures. The turkeys forage for indigenous grasses and insects and are given organic whole grains on a free-choice basis. The flavor of the meat is richer and gamier than the broad-breasted breed of turkeys. For those especially fond of dark meat, these turkeys are succulent. A roast heritage turkey has graced my Thanksgiving table for the last several years. I do recommend brining these birds. Heritage turkeys can often be purchased at farmers' markets and specialty butcher shops, or online at *www.heritagefoodsusa.com*.

"WILD" TURKEYS The only way you are going to get a true wild turkey is to shoot one yourself or cultivate a friend who hunts. Most turkeys labeled "wild" by specialty producers are actually farm raised. These turkeys are expensive, the meat tends to be tough, and the flavor doesn't justify the price. Smile if a friend calls with one freshly killed and cleaned; roast the breast meat and stew the dark meat.

FRESH OR FROZEN? Whether the bird is fresh or frozen, it takes planning when it comes to buying a turkey. Buying a fresh turkey, especially a free-range one, requires a call to the butcher shop or grocery store at least one and often two or more weeks ahead. Obviously, stores like to know how much to order from the turkey producers, though I'm sure they pad their orders for the last minute, yikes-I-forgot-to-order-a-turkey shoppers. However, you can't assume there will be a high-quality turkey waiting for you, so mark your calendar.

The bottom line is: A fresh turkey is a better product overall. First off, the convenience of not having to thaw a turkey for 4 to 5 days in the refrigerator is considerable; turkeys take up a lot of fridge space—usually an entire shelf—and that can be a burden on the cook, the household, and the machine itself. Second, the less time you spend juggling shelf space and monitoring the defrosting turkey, the better. Finally, fresh turkeys are moister, because the freezing process inevitably dries the meat out somewhat.

If, for whatever reason—price, convenience, timing, a supermarket freebie—you select a frozen turkey, you still need to plan ahead. The turkey may be at home with you, but it needs to be thawed carefully and slowly in the refrigerator for several days. If you're short on time, a turkey can be thawed in a sink or very large bowl filled with cold water, but that still takes a whole day. See the chart on page 70 for defrosting times for both of these methods.

Defrosting a Turkey

To defrost a turkey in the refrigerator: Place the frozen turkey, still in its original wrappings, in a large pan with sides. Refrigerate until thawed according to the chart below.

To defrost a turkey in a water bath: Fill a sink or large bowl with cold water. Place the frozen turkey, still in its original wrappings, in the water. Add water as needed to cover the turkey as much as possible. Thaw, changing the water occasionally, according to the chart below.

DEFROSTING TIMES

Weight	In the Refrigerator	In Water
10–12 lbs	2 days	4–6 hours
12–14 lbs	3 days	6–9 hours
14–18 lbs	4 days	9–14 hours
18 lbs & over	4–5 days	14–24 hours

THE RIGHT SIZE TO BUY The size of the turkey you buy depends on several factors, not just the number of people you're feeding. Some of us have ample storage and love to freeze for later meals, make stocks, and so forth. Others of us, not so much—but we do love leftovers. The most obvious concern, of course, is that you want to have enough for everyone at the Thanksgiving table. For turkeys weighing less than 12 pounds, figure on 1 pound of turkey per person; this allows for a reasonable amount of seconds or leftovers. Turkeys weighing more than 12 pounds have more meat per pound, so figure on ¾ to 1 pound per person, which will leave room for plenty of seconds and leftovers.

Size is most important when it comes to handling the bird. I have enough work to do on Thanksgiving Day without engaging in a wrestling match with a large turkey, so I avoid buying a turkey weighing over 18 pounds. (Even capable men will admit—or maybe they won't—that maneuvering a hefty turkey is a lot of work.) If you have 25 people coming for dinner, my suggestion is to roast 2 smaller birds.

Another factor, which many people don't think about until it's too late, is that some ovens can't even accommodate a 25-pound bird. Measure and plan. Finally, a big turkey is impressive only if the bird and the cook make it to the dinner table in one piece. One year, while inching it out of an oven barely large enough to accommodate it, I nearly dropped a 22-pound turkey. So my advice comes from experience!

Brining a Turkey

When I wrote my first Thanksgiving book, *The Thanksgiving Table*, brining a turkey was still a novel method for most home cooks. As I traveled the country teaching Thanksgiving cooking classes, I always demonstrated how to brine a turkey and gave the students an opportunity to taste how moist and flavorful a brined turkey could be. Each year, I respond to lots of preholiday e-mail queries about preparing a turkey and inevitably receive lots of post-holiday e-mails thanking me for my suggestions on brining. After brining and cooking several hundred pounds of turkey each November for my classes, I am convinced that brining produces the juiciest and tastiest turkey I have ever eaten.

The Science Behind Brining Poultry

This is when I want food scientists like Harold Magee and Shirley Corriher at my side! I'm not a food scientist by training, but I have read what feels like almost everything ever written on brining poultry and meat, so with that education I will try to explain in very simple terms why it makes sense to brine.

The central challenge of roasting turkey is that there is a greater volume of white meat than dark meat and the breast meat contains a lot less fat than the dark meat. As a result, when you roast the bird, the breast meat takes longer to cook through than the dark meat, and with little fat to keep it tender, the results are often dry, stringy white meat that needs a lot of gravy to make it moist.

Brining involves soaking the turkey for 12 to 24 hours in a balanced water and salt solution with the addition of sugar and flavoring agents such as spices and herbs. Brining makes the meat juicier overall by increasing the amount of liquid inside the cells of the meat. Water alone will not transport moisture into the cells of the meat. A balanced salt solution causes the muscle fibers to swell, allowing the solution (and the flavors contained in it) to flow into the cells. Once the liquid permeates the cell walls, it stays contained within the cell, moistening and seasoning the meat and resulting in a juicier, tastier bird.

Preparing a Turkey for Brining

To prepare a fresh or thawed frozen turkey for brining, place the turkey, still in its original wrappings, in a clean sink. Carefully slit open the plastic wrapper and remove the turkey. Remove the neck and bag of giblets from both the main cavity and neck cavity of the bird. Store them in a covered container in the refrigerator for making gravy. Remove the plastic or metal clip holding the legs together. Pull off and discard any fat pockets from the neck and main cavities of the bird. Trim off the tail, if desired, and store along with the neck and giblets for stock. Rinse the turkey and pat dry thoroughly. Follow one of the methods detailed on pages 72–73 for brining the turkey. (Safety tip: Always sterilize the sink with a light bleach solution after prepping the turkey.)

Two Methods for Brining

I offer two methods for brining: one for the cook who has either a second refrigerator or the room to take 1 or 2 shelves out of the refrigerator in order to allow a tall stockpot or container to fit upright in it, and another for the home cook who has limited refrigerator space.

Ideally, make the brine solution on the Monday before Thanksgiving. Brine your turkey beginning on Tuesday or Tuesday night. Remove it from the brine solution on Wednesday or Wednesday night. Let it rest, uncovered, in the refrigerator for 6 hours or up to overnight. Then, it's ready to roast on Thanksgiving Day.

Method 1: Brining in a Pot or Container

This method involves brining the turkey in a large stockpot or a sterilized, leak-proof container such as a bucket or restaurant-grade storage container. The pot or container needs to stand upright in the refrigerator, which usually requires removing one or two refrigerator shelves.

1 **FRESH OR THAWED FROZEN TURKEY** (12 to 20 pounds), prepared for brining as directed above

1 **STOCKPOT OR STERILIZED, LEAK-PROOF CONTAINER** large enough to hold the turkey (either upright or on its side) with 3 to 4 inches of headroom

1 recipe of either **Juniper Brine** (page 74), **Apple Cider and Ginger Brine** (page 76), **or Honey and Allspice Brine** (page 77)

Place the turkey in the stockpot or container, standing it upright or on its side, however it fits best. Pour the brine over the bird, then add cold water to cover by 1 inch. Cover the container with a lid, aluminum foil, or plastic wrap and refrigerate for at least 12 or up to 24 hours.

Remove the turkey from the brine. Discard the brine and any cured herbs or spices remaining on the bird. (Discard the oranges and ginger if using the Apple Cider Brine.) Rinse the turkey under cold water and pat dry with paper towels. Place the turkey in a large bowl or roasting pan and refrigerate, unwrapped, for at least 6 hours or up to overnight. This allows the skin of the turkey to dry a bit so it is crisp when roasted. The turkey is now ready to be roasted.

Method 2:
Brining in a Bag

This method involves brining the bird in turkey oven bags set in a roasting pan. The roasting pan will fit on 1 shelf in the refrigerator, saving critical space.

2 **TURKEY-SIZE PLASTIC OVEN BAGS** or **BRINING BAGS** (see Cook's Note)

1 **LARGE ROASTING PAN**

1 **FRESH OR THAWED FROZEN TURKEY** (12 to 20 pounds), prepared for brining as directed above

1 recipe of either **Juniper Brine** (page 74), **Apple Cider and Ginger Brine** (page 76), **or Honey and Allspice Brine** (page 77)

Nest 1 plastic oven bag inside the other to create a double thickness (see Cook's Note). Place the double bag, mouth open wide and facing up, in the roasting pan.

Fold back the top one-third of the double bag to make a collar (this helps keep the bags open). Place the turkey inside the double bag. Unfold the collar of the double bag and pour the brine over the bird, then add 2 cups of cold water. Draw up the top of the inner bag, squeezing out as much air as possible, and secure it closed with a twist tie. Do the same with the outer bag. Turn the package so the turkey is breast side down in the roasting pan and refrigerate for at least 12 or up to 24 hours. Turn the turkey 3 or 4 times while it is brining.

Remove the turkey from the brine. Discard the bags, brine, and any cured herbs or spices remaining on the bird. (Discard the oranges and ginger if using the Apple Cider Brine.) Rinse the turkey under cold water and pat dry with paper towels. Place the turkey back in the roasting pan and refrigerate, unwrapped, for at least 6 hours or up to overnight. This resting period allows the skin of the turkey to dry a bit so it is crisp when roasted. The turkey is now ready to be roasted.

COOK'S NOTE   Plastic oven bags (made by Reynolds) are found with other food storage bags at supermarkets. Buy the turkey-size bags. They are food-safe, plus they are big, strong, tear-resistant, and come with twist ties. Do not use plastic garbage bags, as they are not intended for food storage. I use a double thickness of bags as a precautionary measure against leakage. For the same reason, I place the bagged turkey in a roasting pan.

Juniper Brine

MAKES 3½ QUARTS BRINE,
ENOUGH FOR A
10- TO 25-POUND TURKEY

There are two reasons I am very specific about the salt called for in this recipe. First, I want to use a salt that is 100 percent sodium chloride, without any additives such as calcium silicate, an anti-caking agent, or potassium iodide, a nutritional supplement, both of which I find detract from the salt's flavor. Second, salts have widely varying densities; for example, ⅔ cup of Diamond Crystal salt weighs 3 ounces (85 grams) while ⅔ cup of Morton's kosher salt weighs 5.25 ounces (149 grams), and the same volume of Morton's table salt weighs 6.5 ounces (185 grams)—more than double the weight of the Diamond Crystal! As a result, a brine using table salt may be more than twice as salty as one using the same amount of Diamond Crystal. Now readily available in the spice section of most supermarkets and gourmet grocers, Diamond Crystal is packaged in a bright red box with black lettering. You can substitute any brand of salt, as long as it is pure sodium chloride and you use a weight of 3 ounces (irrespective of volume).

⅔ cup (3 ounces or 85 grams) **DIAMOND CRYSTAL BRAND KOSHER SALT**

⅔ cup **SUGAR**

6 **WHOLE CLOVES**

1 teaspoon **JUNIPER BERRIES,** crushed (see Cook's Note)

½ teaspoon **BLACK PEPPERCORNS,** crushed (see Cook's Note)

2 teaspoons **WHOLE ALLSPICE BERRIES,** crushed (see Cook's Note)

5 **FRESH SAGE LEAVES**

4 sprigs **FRESH THYME**

2 **BAY LEAVES**

8 cups **HOT WATER**

4 cups **ICE WATER**

In a large saucepan, stir together the salt, sugar, cloves, juniper berries, peppercorns, and allspice. Add the sage leaves, thyme, and bay leaves along with the hot water. Stir to combine. Bring to a boil over high heat, stirring frequently until the salt and sugar have dissolved. Boil for 3 minutes, then remove from the heat. Add the ice water and stir to cool the mixture. Set aside and let cool to room temperature.

Proceed with brining the turkey (see pages 72–73).

COOK'S NOTE The easiest way to crush whole spices is to use a mortar and pestle or a spice grinder. If you do not have either of these kitchen tools, place the whole spices in a heavy lock-top plastic bag, seal the bag while pressing out all the air, and pound them with the bottom of a small, heavy saucepan until coarsely crushed.

DO AHEAD The brine can be made up to 1 day in advance. Cover and set aside at room temperature.

Apple Cider and Ginger Brine

**MAKES 3½ QUARTS BRINE,
ENOUGH FOR A
10- TO 25-POUND TURKEY**

Please read the headnote for the **Juniper Brine** (page 74) for information regarding Diamond Crystal brand salt. I especially like to use this brine when barbecuing a turkey because the sweet apple cider flavor is a perfect match with the hickory smoke–infused bird.

⅔ cup (3 ounces or 85 grams)
**DIAMOND CRYSTAL BRAND
KOSHER SALT**

⅔ cup **SUGAR**

6 **WHOLE CLOVES**

1 teaspoon **BLACK PEPPERCORNS**,
crushed (see Cook's Note, page 74)

2 teaspoons **WHOLE ALLSPICE
BERRIES**, crushed
(see Cook's Note, page 74)

6 quarter-size slices **FRESH GINGER**

2 **BAY LEAVES**

6 cups **UNSWEETENED APPLE CIDER
OR JUICE**

2 cups **HOT WATER**

4 cups **ICE WATER**

1 large **NAVEL ORANGE**, cut into
8 wedges

In a large saucepan, stir together the salt, sugar, cloves, peppercorns, and allspice. Add the ginger and bay leaves along with the apple cider and hot water. Stir to combine. Bring to a boil over high heat, stirring frequently until the salt and sugar have dissolved. Boil for 3 minutes, then remove from the heat. Add the ice water and orange pieces and stir to cool the mixture. Set aside and let cool to room temperature.

Proceed with brining the turkey (see pages 72–73).

DO AHEAD The brine can be made up to 1 day in advance. Cover and refrigerate until ready to use.

Honey and Allspice Brine

MAKES 3½ QUARTS BRINE,
ENOUGH FOR A
10- TO 25-POUND TURKEY

Please read the headnote for the Juniper Brine (page 74) for information regarding Diamond Crystal brand salt. This brine works wonderfully with either a roasted or barbecued turkey. I especially like to use this brine with the Roast Turkey with Vidalia Cream Gravy on page 99.

8 cups **HOT WATER**

⅔ cup (3 ounces or 85 grams) **DIAMOND CRYSTAL BRAND KOSHER SALT**

1 cup **HONEY**

6 **WHOLE CLOVES**

1 teaspoon **BLACK PEPPERCORNS**, crushed (see Cook's Note, page 74)

2 teaspoons **WHOLE ALLSPICE BERRIES**, crushed (see Cook's Note, page 74)

2 **BAY LEAVES**

4 sprigs **FRESH THYME**

4 cups **ICE WATER**

In a large saucepan, combine 2 cups of the hot water with the salt, honey, cloves, peppercorns, and allspice. Add the bay leaves and thyme along with the remaining hot water. Stir to combine. Bring to a boil over high heat, stirring frequently until the salt has dissolved. Boil for 3 minutes, then remove from the heat. Add the ice water and stir to cool the mixture. Set aside and let cool to room temperature.

Proceed with brining the turkey (see pages 72–73).

DO AHEAD The brine can be made up to 1 day in advance. Cover and refrigerate until ready to use.

Turkey Stock for Gravy

MAKES ABOUT 3 CUPS This is the simplest way I know to make a rich turkey stock, utilizing the turkey neck, tail, gizzard, and heart found inside the neck cavity of the turkey. (I never use the liver, also found in the packet of giblets, for making stock, because it gives the stock a bitter flavor. I cook the liver separately, chop it, and add it to my stuffing.)

To make a bigger batch of stock, to cook ahead and freeze, use about 5 pounds of turkey wings, thighs, or drumsticks in place of the giblets and turkey neck listed in this recipe and double the quantities of the rest of the ingredients. Brown the turkey parts in a roasting pan in a preheated 400°F oven for 1½ hours. Transfer them to a stockpot and proceed with the recipe, starting after the browning step.

2 tablespoons **CANOLA OIL**

TURKEY NECK, TAIL, GIZZARD, AND HEART

1 **YELLOW ONION**, root end trimmed but peel left intact, quartered

1 large **CARROT**, scrubbed but not peeled, cut into 2-inch chunks

1 large rib **CELERY** including leafy tops, trimmed and cut into 2-inch lengths

2 sprigs **FRESH THYME**

4 sprigs **FRESH PARSLEY**

1 **BAY LEAF**

6 **BLACK PEPPERCORNS**

2 cups **CANNED LOW-SODIUM CHICKEN BROTH**

5 cups **COLD WATER**

In a large saucepan, heat the oil over medium heat. Add the turkey neck, tail, gizzard, and heart and sauté until browned on all sides, 5 to 7 minutes. Add the onion, carrot, celery, thyme, parsley, bay leaf, peppercorns, chicken broth, and water to the pan. Bring to a boil over medium-high heat, then reduce the heat to low. Skim any brown foam that rises to the top. Simmer the stock until it reduces by half, about 1 hour. Pour the stock through a fine-mesh sieve set over a bowl or 4-cup glass measure. Set aside the neck, gizzard, and heart until cool enough to handle. Discard the rest of the solids. Let the stock cool completely. Skim off any fat that rises to the top. Cover and refrigerate until ready to use. (When you're ready to make gravy, skim the fat from the top of the stock again, if necessary.)

If making giblet gravy, shred the meat from the neck and finely dice the gizzard and heart. Cover and refrigerate until you are ready to use. (Some cooks prefer to make a smooth gravy and add the diced gizzard and heart to their stuffing.)

DO AHEAD The turkey stock can be made up to 2 days in advance. Let cool completely, cover, and refrigerate. Refrigerate the neck, gizzard, and heart in a separate covered container. If making a large batch of stock from purchased turkey parts, the stock can be made up to 1 month in advance and frozen in airtight containers.

Trussing, Roasting Times, Carving, and Presentation

Trussing a Turkey

Trussing a turkey means nothing more than securing the bird with string, skewers, or poultry pins in order to keep its limbs primly in place. This is basically a presentation issue. The turkey looks prettier with its wings tucked in close to the breast and its legs demurely closed. And, honestly, it is easier to turn the turkey while roasting it when it is securely tied. I own a trussing needle but almost never use it. It is easy, and quite effective, just to tie the bird with some kitchen twine (see page 16) using the methods detailed below. Though I prefer to roast an unstuffed turkey (because I like stuffing as a side dish that is crispy and beautifully browned on top), here are directions for trussing both a stuffed and unstuffed bird, plus a hybrid trussing method.

TO TRUSS AN UNSTUFFED TURKEY Have ready one 4-feet length of kitchen twine. Place the turkey, breast side up, on a work surface with the legs facing you. Arrange the flap of neck skin so it covers the neck cavity. Center the twine across the back (on the work surface) under the shoulders of the turkey, making sure it secures the neck skin. With an end in each hand, pull the string up over the top of the breast, tightening it so the wings are drawn in close to the body; then cross over the two ends and tie. Now bring the twine down to the legs, bring the legs together, wrap the string around the ends (knobs) of the legs, and tie a knot. Trim any extra length of string.

TO TRUSS A STUFFED TURKEY Have ready one 4-foot length of kitchen twine and one 1-foot length, plus 4 or 5 thin metal skewers or poultry pins. Loosely fill both the neck and main cavities with stuffing. Stuffing expands when heated, which is why you don't want it packed in the cavities. Put any extra stuffing in a buttered baking pan and bake it separately. The stuffing should be at room temperature. Cold stuffing, when packed inside the turkey, may not reach 165°F (the temperature it needs to reach to avoid harmful bacteria from developing) by the time the turkey is done.

Pull the flap of neck skin over the stuffed neck cavity and secure it to the body with a skewer. Now pull the skin together on either side of the chest cavity and close it securely with 3 or 4 skewers. Using the short piece of twine, tie a knot around the tail. Lace the twine up the skewers, from bottom to top, as if lacing a shoe; then knot the ends of the string together. Cut off the excess string. Use the 4-feet length to tie the rest of the bird as directed in the instructions for trussing an unstuffed turkey.

QUICK TRUSSING METHOD The simplest way to keep a turkey contained without a lot of fuss, whether the turkey is stuffed or unstuffed, is to tie the legs together with kitchen twine so they hold their shape, and to tuck the wing tips under, bending the wing tip back and under the second wing joint.

Roasting Times for a Brined Turkey

The times listed below are based on an oven temperature of 500°F for the first 30 minutes, and 350°F for the remainder of the roasting time. The turkey is roasted (using a V-shaped roasting rack) breast side down for 1 hour, then turned and roasted breast side up for the remainder of the cooking time. This method produces an evenly browned, beautiful turkey with crisp skin and moist meat. The turkey is done when an instant-read meat thermometer inserted into the thickest part of the thigh registers 160° to 165°F. Let the turkey rest, tented with aluminum foil to keep it warm, for 30 to 45 minutes before carving. (The internal temperature will rise 5 to 10 degrees while the turkey rests.) The resting time allows the poultry juices to be drawn back into the meat, keeping the bird moist and firm when it comes time to carve.

Weight	Unstuffed Turkey	Stuffed Turkey
10–12 lbs	1¾–2 hours	2–2¼ hours
12–14 lbs	2–2½ hours	2¼–3 hours
14–18 lbs	2½–3 hours	2¾–3½ hours
18 lbs & over	3 hours+	4 hours+

Carving a Turkey

If you are a confident turkey carver, place the turkey on a large serving platter and carve it at the table. For the majority of us, carving the turkey in the kitchen is a safer bet. Place the turkey on a carving board, ideally one that has a moat and well to catch the delicious poultry juices. Untie the bird and remove the skewers, if you used them. Using a sharp carving knife and meat fork, cut down between the thigh and body until you feel bone. Twist and pull down on the leg and thigh a little until you see the thigh joint. Now cut through the joint to separate the thigh from the body. Cut the joint where the leg meets the thigh. Repeat on the other side. Now you have legs and thighs ready for a warm platter.

To carve the breast meat, start at the keel bone that runs along the top of the breast. Angle the knife and cut thin slices of breast meat from one side of the bird. Continue until you reach the rib cage; then carve the other breast. (Alternatively, some carvers prefer to cut the entire side of the breast from the bone and then slice the breast on an angle into thick slices.) At this point you should have plenty of meat for serving. Lay slices of breast meat in an overlapping fashion down the center of the platter. Place the legs and thighs along the side. If a guest wants to have a wing, pull back the wing until you see the joint between the wing and the body, cut through that joint, and add the wing to the platter. Cover the rest of the turkey loosely with aluminum foil and remove the rest of the meat from the carcass later for some fine leftovers.

PRESENTATION When considering presentation, the question you have to ask yourself is: Do you want drama or ease of serving for Thanksgiving dinner? There is no right or wrong answer; it's a matter of what you are comfortable with. Presenting a whole roasted bird on a large, artfully garnished platter is a showstopper on a buffet or at the head of a dining table. Just remember, you'll need to study the section on carving so you know what you are doing, and have an attractive carving set (a sharp carving knife and carving fork) ready for the task at hand. Play the part, and carve with authority and confidence. It's fun.

If you want to carve the turkey in the kitchen and present a platter of meat to guests, follow the carving directions, and garnish one corner of the platter or two corners diagonally opposite each other with some of the garnishes suggested below. Keep it simple; the presentation of fanned-out, overlapping turkey slices is beautiful in itself.

GARNISHES I always like my garnishes to relate to the dish being garnished. For instance, when I make the Herb Butter–Rubbed Turkey with Giblet Gravy (page 96), I buy or snip from the garden extra bunches of fresh sage, thyme, and parsley. You can either tuck the herbs around the base of the bird or place them at the corners of the platter. For the Maple-Glazed Roast Turkey with Applejack Giblet Gravy (page 92), fresh herbs look great as a garnish, and so do lady apples and kumquats nestled on top of the herbs.

See what's in your garden, if you have one. Interesting greens like kale or savoy cabbage make beautiful garnishes. A quick trip to the yard and a few snips with a scissors is all it takes. If you don't have a garden, peruse the produce aisles of your market for interesting seasonal produce. If the platter is large enough, small gourds and Indian corn nestled on herbs or greens look pretty around the edges of a serving platter. Just avoid the clichés—curly-leaf parsley with slices of orange, or parsley with pickled crabapples—and your turkey will look regal and festive.

Juniper-Brined Roast Turkey with Chanterelle Mushroom Gravy

SERVES 12 TO 20, DEPENDING ON THE SIZE OF THE TURKEY

Living in the Pacific Northwest, with our bounty of berries, tree-ripened fruits, hazelnuts, and wild mushrooms, makes going to the farmers' market feel like a season-long treasure hunt. I'm especially rewarded when I stop at the mushroom forager's stand and see a basket chock-full of chanterelle mushrooms. At the peak of the season, I buy fresh chanterelles and use them as often as I can, as in this golden-hued mushroom gravy accompaniment to the holiday bird.

1 large **YELLOW ONION**, chopped

1 large **CARROT**, peeled and chopped

1 large rib **CELERY**, chopped

2 cloves **GARLIC**, minced

7 **FRESH SAGE LEAVES**, chopped

1 tablespoon **FRESH THYME LEAVES**

Freshly ground **PEPPER**

One 12- to 16-pound **BRINED TURKEY** (see pages 72–73) made with **Juniper Brine** (page 74)

½ cup (1 stick) **UNSALTED BUTTER**, melted

Chanterelle Mushroom Gravy (page 85)

Combine the onion, carrot, celery, garlic, sage, thyme, and a few grinds of pepper in a medium bowl. Mix well and set aside.

Position a rack on the second-lowest level in the oven and preheat to 500°F. Have ready a large roasting pan with a roasting rack, preferably V-shaped, set in the pan.

Put ½ cup of the vegetable mixture inside the neck cavity and ½ cup inside the chest cavity of the turkey. Scatter the remainder on the bottom of the roasting pan and add 1 cup water to the pan. Truss the turkey, following the directions for trussing an unstuffed turkey on page 79. Using a pastry brush, brush the turkey with half of the melted butter. Place the turkey, breast side down, on the roasting rack. Roast for 30 minutes, then reduce the oven temperature to 350°F. Baste the turkey with the pan juices and roast for 30 minutes longer.

● ● CONTINUED ● ●

Juniper-Brined Roast Turkey with Chanterelle
Mushroom Gravy

Remove the turkey from the oven. Using silicone oven mitts, regular oven mitts covered with aluminum foil, or wads of paper towels, turn the turkey breast side up. (It won't be very hot at this point.) Baste with the pan juices and the remaining melted butter, and return the turkey to the oven. Continue to roast, basting with the pan juices again after 45 minutes. At this point, check the internal temperature of the turkey by inserting an instant-read thermometer into the thickest part of a thigh without touching bone. (As a point of reference, when the internal temperature of the turkey reaches 125°F, the turkey is about 1 hour away from being done. Of course, roasting times will vary, depending on the size of the bird, its temperature when it went into the oven, whether or not it is stuffed, and your particular oven and the accuracy of the thermostat. See the chart on page 80 for guidance.) The turkey is done when the instant-read thermometer registers 160° to 165°F when inserted into the thickest part of a thigh away from the bone.

When the turkey is done, tilt the body so the juices from the main cavity run into the pan. Transfer to a carving board or serving platter and cover loosely with aluminum foil. Let the turkey rest for 30 to 40 minutes before carving, to allow the juices to redistribute. (The internal temperature will rise 5 to 10 degrees while the turkey rests.)

Strain the juices, vegetables, and browned bits from the roasting pan through a fine-mesh sieve set over a large glass measuring cup. Set aside and allow the fat to rise to the top. Spoon off the fat. The pan juices from a brined turkey are usually too salty to add to gravy, so I refrigerate them and add to the water for making stock from the carcass; the juices provide additional flavor and the salt is diluted by the water. See After-Thanksgiving Turkey Stock, page 190.

Carve the turkey, following the directions on page 80. Serve, accompanied by the Chanterelle Mushroom Gravy.

Chanterelle Mushroom Gravy

MAKES ABOUT 3 CUPS

This gravy can be made while the turkey roasts. If chanterelle mushrooms are not available, substitute other fresh wild mushrooms, use cremini mushrooms, or buy dried chanterelle mushrooms and soak them in warm water to rehydrate before adding to the gravy. If you are serving a few vegetarians for Thanksgiving, you could make an additional half-recipe of this gravy using a rich homemade or canned vegetable broth.

4 tablespoons (½ stick)
UNSALTED BUTTER

1 **SHALLOT**, minced

¾ pound **CHANTERELLE MUSHROOMS**, wiped or brushed clean and finely chopped

¼ cup **INSTANT FLOUR** such as Wondra or Shake & Blend

3 cups **Turkey Stock for Gravy** (page 78)

KOSHER OR SEA SALT

Freshly ground **WHITE PEPPER**

In a 2½-quart saucepan over medium heat, melt the butter and swirl to coat the pan. Add the shallot and sauté until soft but not browned, about 1 minute. Add the mushrooms and sauté, stirring frequently, until the mushrooms soften and give up their juices, about 5 minutes.

Meanwhile, in a small bowl or measuring cup, whisk together the flour and ½ cup of the stock until the flour is dissolved.

Add the remaining 2½ cups stock to the mushrooms in the pan and bring to a simmer. Whisk in the flour mixture and simmer until the gravy thickens, about 5 minutes. Taste and adjust the seasoning with salt and pepper. Keep warm until ready to serve.

DO AHEAD

The gravy can be made up to 1 day in advance. Cover and refrigerate. Reheat gently just before serving.

Spatchcocked Turkey Roasted with Lemon, Sage, and Garlic

SERVES 8 TO 12, DEPENDING ON THE SIZE OF THE TURKEY

Spatchcock, an old culinary term of Irish origin, is an abbreviation of "dispatch cock," a phrase used to describe preparing a bird by splitting it down the back, spreading it open like a book, and pressing it flat for easy, faster roasting. I could have also used the term *butterflied*.

Keep in mind that this turkey will not look like a Norman Rockwell image of a perfectly roasted turkey presented on a platter. It is meant to be carved in the kitchen. The turkey is spread open and roasted flat to speed up the cooking time. Once carved and presented on an elegant platter, you won't be able to tell the difference between a spatchcocked turkey and one you have roasted whole. This method is brilliant for the Thanksgiving cook with little time to prepare and cook, because a 10- to 14-pound turkey will roast in about an hour and a half. I promise that butterflying the turkey is not difficult, especially if you have poultry shears or a sharp chef's knife.

6 cloves **GARLIC**

Zest of 1 **LEMON**, removed in ½-inch-wide strips

10 large **SAGE LEAVES**, coarsely chopped

1 tablespoon **FRESH THYME LEAVES**

1 teaspoon **KOSHER OR SEA SALT**, plus more for seasoning

1 teaspoon freshly ground **PEPPER**, plus more for seasoning

1 cup (2 sticks) **UNSALTED BUTTER** at room temperature, cut into chunks

One 10- to 14-pound **FRESH OR THAWED FROZEN TURKEY** (see page 69), removed from the refrigerator 1 hour before roasting

Giblet Gravy for a Spatchcocked Turkey (page 89)

Position a rack on the second-lowest level in the oven and preheat to 350°F. Have ready a roasting pan large enough to accommodate the turkey when laid flat after spatchcocking (butterflying).

In a food processor fitted with the metal blade, combine the garlic, lemon zest, sage, thyme, salt, and pepper. Process until finely minced. Add the butter and process until well combined.

Place the turkey, still in its original wrappings, in a clean sink. Carefully slit open the plastic wrapper and remove the turkey. Remove the neck and bag of giblets from both the main cavity and neck cavity of the bird. Store them in a covered container in the refrigerator for making the gravy. Remove the plastic or metal clip holding the legs together. Pull and discard any fat pockets from the neck and main cavities of the bird. Trim off the tail, if desired, and store along with the neck and giblets for stock. Rinse the turkey and pat dry thoroughly.

●● CONTINUED ●●

To butterfly the turkey, place it, breast down, on a cutting board. Using poultry shears or a chef's knife, cut through the turkey from one end to the other on each side of the backbone to remove it. Cut the backbone in half and refrigerate it for making stock for gravy. Turn the turkey breast side up, pull the body open, and use the heel of your hand to press down firmly, cracking the rib bones so the turkey lies flat. This takes a little pressure and strength; you might need to make a partial cut through the breastbone to get the turkey to lie flat.

Using your fingers, and being careful not to tear the skin, loosen the skin from the breast of the turkey to create a pocket. Smear the lemon-herb butter all over the breast meat under the skin with your fingers, pushing some butter over the thigh and leg meat. Rub the skin of the turkey all over with any remaining flavored butter and season on all sides with salt and pepper. Transfer to the roasting pan, laying the turkey out flat, skin side up. Roast for about 1½ hours, depending on the size of the bird, until an instant-read thermometer registers 160° to 165°F when inserted into the thickest part of the thigh. Make the giblet gravy while the turkey is roasting.

Transfer the turkey to a carving board and cover loosely with aluminum foil. Let rest for 20 minutes before carving, to allow the juices to redistribute. (The internal temperature will rise 5 to 10 degrees while the turkey rests.) Finish making the gravy while the turkey is resting.

Strain the juices and browned bits from the roasting pan through a fine-mesh sieve set over a large glass measuring cup. Set aside and allow the fat to rise to the top. Spoon off the fat. The pan juices can be added to the gravy.

Carve the turkey, following the directions on page 80. Serve, accompanied by the Giblet Gravy.

Giblet Gravy for a Spatchcocked Turkey

MAKES ABOUT 3½ CUPS

This gravy gets deep flavor from adding the turkey backbone to the stock along with the neck and giblets. Make the stock and strain it while the turkey roasts.

3 tablespoons **VEGETABLE OIL**

TURKEY BACKBONE, NECK, TAIL, GIZZARD, AND HEART

1 **YELLOW ONION**, root end trimmed but peel left intact, quartered

1 large **CARROT**, scrubbed but not peeled, cut into 2-inch chunks

1 large rib **CELERY** including leafy tops, trimmed and cut into 2-inch lengths

2 sprigs **FRESH THYME**

4 sprigs **FRESH PARSLEY**

1 **BAY LEAF**

6 **BLACK PEPPERCORNS**

2 cups **CANNED LOW-SODIUM CHICKEN BROTH**

5 cups **COLD WATER**

¼ cup **INSTANT FLOUR** such as Wondra or Shake & Blend

KOSHER OR SEA SALT

Freshly ground **PEPPER**

Begin the gravy by first making a turkey stock. In a large saucepan, heat the oil over medium heat. Add the turkey parts and sauté until browned on all sides, 5 to 7 minutes. Add the onion, carrot, celery, thyme, parsley, bay leaf, peppercorns, chicken broth, and water to the pan. Bring to a boil over medium-high heat, then reduce the heat to low. Skim any brown foam that rises to the top. Simmer the stock until it reduces by half, about 1 hour. Pour the stock through a fine-mesh strainer set over a bowl or 4-cup glass measure. Set aside the neck, back, gizzard, and heart until cool enough to handle. Discard the rest of the solids. Set the stock aside, and when the fat rises to the top, skim it off. Shred the meat from the neck and back and set aside. Finely dice the gizzard and heart and set aside.

Meanwhile, in a small bowl or measuring cup, whisk together the flour and ½ cup of the strained turkey stock until the flour is dissolved.

Stir the reserved defatted juices from the roasting pan into the turkey stock. Measure 3 cups of the stock and pour it into a medium saucepan. Bring to a simmer over medium-high heat. Whisk in the flour mixture and simmer until the gravy thickens, about 5 minutes. Add the reserved gizzard and heart along with a portion of the shredded meat, just enough to enrich the gravy. Taste and adjust the seasoning with salt and pepper. Transfer to a warmed gravy boat or bowl and serve immediately.

Hickory Grill-Roasted Turkey

SERVES 12 TO 20, DEPENDING ON THE SIZE OF THE TURKEY

Grill-roasting a turkey is a guaranteed show-stopping, big-flavored way to cook a turkey, and the hickory-smoked turkey leftovers are divine. From a practical side, if you are a one-oven household, barbecuing your Thanksgiving bird is the best way to free up oven space for all those pans of stuffing, sweet potatoes, and gratin that need to be baked. In addition, there is no messy roasting pan or grease-splattered oven to clean up. It is a delightful cooking method for those living in a warm climate, and for those diehards who light up a grill whether it's raining or snowing, the can-do spirit will prevail, because barbecuing a turkey is easy. Make the **Applejack Giblet Gravy** (page 95) if you like; it is amazing with a barbecued bird. Another option is to use your favorite bottled barbecue sauce. Allow 12 to 24 hours for brining the bird before you start cooking.

This grill recipe uses a technique called "indirect cooking" or "indirect-heat grilling." This simply means that the food is not set directly over the coals or burners as it cooks in a covered grill. Essentially, this is grill-roasting—the heat rises and circulates by reflecting off the lid and sides of the grill. Indirect-heat grilling is used for long, slow cooking; it is the best method for barbecuing whole chickens, roasts, ribs, and turkeys. Directions are given for both a gas grill and a charcoal-burning, kettle-style grill with a vented lid.

Special Equipment

6 to 8 cups **HICKORY CHIPS**

KITCHEN TWINE

STURDY, V-SHAPED ROASTING RACK (see page 17)

HEAVY-GAUGE, DISPOSABLE FOIL ROASTING PAN large enough to hold the roasting rack

HEAVY-DUTY ALUMINUM FOIL OR A DISPOSABLE ALUMINUM PIE PLATE

About 1 hour before you are ready to grill, place the hickory chips in a large bowl, cover with cold water, and soak. In the meantime, secure the legs of the turkey with a 1-foot length of kitchen twine by bringing the legs together, wrapping the string around the ends (knobs) of the legs, and then tying the string with a knot. Trim any extra length of string. Rub or lightly brush the turkey with olive oil. Place the bird, breast side down, on the roasting rack, and set it inside the disposable roasting pan.

One 12- to 16-pound **BRINED TURKEY** (see pages 72–73) made with **Apple Cider and Ginger Brine** (page 76)

OLIVE OIL for brushing the turkey (about ½ cup)

Applejack Giblet Gravy (page 95) or barbecue sauce for serving

Drain the soaking hickory chips. Make 3 aluminum foil pouches or use 1 disposable foil pie plate. (Skip this step if your gas grill has a smoker box, and follow the manufacturer's instructions for using wood chips.) To make the pouches, cut three 16-inch-long pieces of heavy-duty foil. Fold each in half to make a pouch about 8 inches long, and fill with one-third of the wood chips. Crimp the edges together to seal and poke a few holes in the top of the pouch. If using a small disposable foil pie plate, fill it with one-third of the chips.

FOR A CHARCOAL GRILL About 45 minutes prior to grilling, prepare a hardwood charcoal or charcoal briquette fire. When the coals are covered with a gray ash, mound them on one side of the grill. Place 1 pouch or the pie plate of wood chips directly on the coals. Place the roasting pan on the side of the cooking grate away from the coals. Close the grill lid.

FOR A GAS GRILL About 20 minutes prior to grilling, preheat the grill to high with all the burners on. When the grill is hot, turn off the burner directly below where the turkey will sit and adjust the other burner(s) to medium-high. Place the drained wood chips in the smoker box, or place 1 pouch or the pie plate of wood chips directly on the heat source. Place the roasting pan on the cooking grate on the side of the gas grill that has been turned off. Close the grill lid.

Grill-roast the turkey for 1 hour. Open the grill lid. Add more wood chips if needed. With a wad of paper towels in each hand, turn the turkey, breast side up, and arrange it so the leg and wing facing the fire are now facing away from it. Continue cooking, with the lid closed, for another 45 minutes.

Check the wood chips and add more, if needed. Turn the turkey once again so the leg and wing facing the fire are now facing away from it. Continue cooking, with the lid closed, for another 45 minutes. At this point, check the internal temperature of the turkey by inserting an instant-read thermometer into the thickest part of a thigh without touching bone. Check both thighs. When the thermometer registers 160° to 165°F in both thighs, the turkey is done.

Transfer the turkey to a carving board and cover loosely with aluminum foil. Let the turkey rest for 30 minutes to allow the juices to distribute. Carve the turkey, following the directions on page 80. Serve accompanied by a sauceboat of gravy or barbecue sauce.

Maple-Glazed Roast Turkey with Applejack Giblet Gravy

SERVES 12 TO 20, DEPENDING ON THE SIZE OF THE TURKEY

This burnished, maple-glazed roast turkey combines all the luscious fall flavors of New England—crisp apples, pure maple syrup, and, in the Yankee spirit, a gravy spiked with applejack brandy. I like to pair this turkey with either Sourdough Stuffing with Roasted Chestnuts and Apples (page 116) or New England Bread Stuffing with Bell's Seasoning (page 122).

1 large **YELLOW ONION**, quartered

4 cloves **GARLIC**

2 **GOLDEN DELICIOUS APPLES**, cored and quartered

4 sprigs **FRESH THYME**

4 **FRESH SAGE LEAVES**

One 12- to 16-pound **BRINED TURKEY** (see pages 72–73) made with **Apple Cider and Ginger Brine** (page 76)

6 tablespoons (¾ stick) **UNSALTED BUTTER**, melted

Freshly ground **PEPPER**

1 cup **HOMEMADE CHICKEN STOCK** (see page 11) **OR CANNED LOW-SODIUM CHICKEN BROTH**

1 cup **APPLE CIDER**

½ cup **PURE MAPLE SYRUP**

Applejack Giblet Gravy (page 95)

Position a rack on the second-lowest level in the oven and preheat to 500°F. Have ready a large roasting pan with a roasting rack, preferably V-shaped, set in the pan.

Place the onion, garlic, apples, thyme, and sage inside the chest cavity of the turkey. Truss the turkey, following the directions for trussing an unstuffed turkey on page 79. Using a pastry brush, brush the turkey with the butter. Season the turkey with a few grinds of freshly ground pepper. Place the turkey, breast side down, on the roasting rack. Add the stock and apple cider to the pan. Roast for 30 minutes. Reduce the oven temperature to 350°F. Baste the turkey with the pan juices and roast for 30 minutes longer.

Remove the turkey from the oven. Using silicone oven mitts, regular oven mitts covered with aluminum foil, or wads of paper towels, turn the turkey breast side up. (It won't be very hot at this point.) Baste with the pan juices and return the turkey to the oven. Continue to roast, basting with the pan juices again after 45 minutes. At this point, check the internal temperature of the turkey by inserting an instant-read thermometer into the thickest part of a thigh without touching bone. (As a point of reference, when the internal temperature of the turkey reaches 125°F, the turkey is about 1 hour away from being done. Of course, roasting times will vary, depending on the size of the bird, its temperature when it went into the oven, whether or not it is stuffed, and your particular oven and the accuracy of the thermostat. See the chart on page 80 for guidance.)

•• CONTINUED ••

During the last 20 minutes of roasting, brush the turkey with the maple syrup. Return the turkey to the oven and continue to roast until the instant-read thermometer registers 160° to 165°F when inserted into the thickest part of the thigh without touching bone.

When the turkey is done, tilt the body so the juices from the main cavity run into the pan. Transfer the turkey to a carving board or serving platter and cover loosely with aluminum foil. Let the turkey rest for 30 to 40 minutes before carving, to allow the juices to redistribute. (The internal temperature will rise 5 to 10 degrees while the turkey rests.)

Carve the turkey, following the directions on page 80. Serve, accompanied by the Applejack Giblet Gravy.

Applejack Giblet Gravy

MAKES ABOUT 3½ CUPS

A touch of applejack spikes the flavor of this gravy, adding a subtle hint of the fermented and distilled, tree-ripened apples. It's a terrific complement to the apple cider–brined turkey.

2 tablespoons **UNSALTED BUTTER**

COOKED HEART, GIZZARD, AND NECK MEAT from the **Turkey Stock for Gravy** (page 78), finely minced

¼ cup **INSTANT FLOUR** such as Wondra or Shake & Blend

2½ cups **Turkey Stock for Gravy** (page 78)

¼ cup **APPLEJACK BRANDY**, or more to taste

KOSHER OR SEA SALT

Freshly ground **PEPPER**

In a saucepan over medium heat, melt the butter and swirl to coat the pan. Add the minced heart, gizzard, and neck meat and sauté until heated through, about 1 minute.

Meanwhile, in a small bowl or measuring cup, whisk together the flour and ½ cup of the stock until the flour is dissolved.

Add the remaining 2 cups stock to the pan and bring to a simmer. Whisk in the flour mixture and simmer until the gravy thickens, about 5 minutes. Stir in the applejack. Season to taste with salt and pepper. Add more applejack, if desired. Keep warm until ready to serve.

DO AHEAD The gravy can be made up to 1 day in advance. Cover and refrigerate. Reheat gently just before serving.

Herb Butter–Rubbed Turkey with Giblet Gravy

SERVES 12 TO 20, DEPENDING ON THE SIZE OF THE TURKEY

One of my favorite ways to roast a chicken is to tuck fresh herbs and butter under the breast skin and stuff the cavity with onion, garlic, and more fresh herbs. This is a classic French technique; why not adapt it to our American turkey and have a beautiful, buttery, Thanksgiving bird? Stuffing the cavity with aromatics infuses the turkey with savory flavors. Either the **Sourdough Stuffing with Roasted Chestnuts and Apples** (page 116) or the **Linguiça Sausage Stuffing with Mushrooms and Caramelized Onions** (page 119) would be a fabulous accompaniment. Bake the stuffing separately so it is crispy on top and wonderfully browned.

1 large **YELLOW ONION**, quartered

4 cloves **GARLIC**

12 **FRESH SAGE LEAVES**

4 sprigs **FRESH THYME**, plus 2 tablespoons fresh thyme leaves

4 sprigs **FRESH FLAT-LEAF PARSLEY**

One 12- to 16-pound **BRINED TURKEY** (see pages 72–73) made with **Juniper Brine** (page 74)

¾ cup (1½ sticks) **UNSALTED BUTTER**, melted

Freshly ground **PEPPER**

1½ cups **HOMEMADE CHICKEN STOCK** (see page 11) **OR CANNED LOW-SODIUM CHICKEN BROTH**

Giblet Gravy (page 98)

Position a rack on the second-lowest level in the oven and preheat to 500°F. Have ready a large roasting pan with a roasting rack, preferably V-shaped, set in the pan.

Place the onion, garlic, 4 of the sage leaves, and the 4 thyme and parsley sprigs inside the chest cavity of the turkey. Mince the 8 remaining sage leaves and combine them with the 2 tablespoons thyme leaves and ½ cup of the melted butter in a small bowl.

At the top of the turkey breast, slide your fingers back and forth under the skin to separate it from the breast meat, creating a pocket over the entire breast. Pour the herb-butter mixture inside this pocket. Truss the turkey following the directions for quick trussing a turkey on page 79. Using a pastry brush, brush the turkey with the remaining ¼ cup butter. Season the turkey with a few grinds of freshly ground pepper. Place the turkey, breast side down, on the roasting rack. Add the stock to the pan. Roast for 30 minutes, then reduce the oven temperature to 350°F. Baste the turkey with the pan juices and roast for 30 minutes longer.

Remove the turkey from the oven. Using silicone oven mitts, regular oven mitts covered with aluminum foil, or wads of paper towels, turn the turkey breast side up. (It won't be very hot at this point.) Baste with the pan juices and return the turkey to the oven. Continue to roast, basting with the pan juices again after 45 minutes. At this point, check the internal temperature of the turkey by inserting an instant-read thermometer into the thickest part of a thigh without touching bone. (As a point of reference, when the internal temperature of the turkey reaches 125°F, the turkey is about 1 hour away from being done. Of course, roasting times will vary, depending on the size of the bird, its temperature when it went into the oven, whether or not it is stuffed, and your particular oven and the accuracy of the thermostat. See the chart on page 80 for guidance.) The turkey is done when the instant-read thermometer registers 160° to 165°F when inserted into the thickest part of the thigh away from the bone.

When the turkey is done, tilt the body so the juices from the main cavity run into the pan. Transfer to a carving board or serving platter and cover loosely with aluminum foil. Let the turkey rest for 30 to 40 minutes before carving, to allow the juices to redistribute. (The internal temperature will rise 5 to 10 degrees while the turkey rests.)

Strain the juices, herbs, and browned bits from the roasting pan through a fine-mesh sieve set over a large glass measuring cup. Set aside and allow the fat to rise to the top. Spoon off the fat. The pan juices from a brined turkey are usually too salty to add to gravy, so I refrigerate them and add to the water for making stock from the carcass; the juices provide additional flavor and the salt is diluted by the water. See After-Thanksgiving Turkey Stock, page 190.

Carve the turkey, following the directions on page 80. Serve, accompanied by the Giblet Gravy.

Giblet Gravy

MAKES ABOUT 3½ CUPS This is perhaps the most traditional gravy served at Thanksgiving.

2 tablespoons **UNSALTED BUTTER**

COOKED HEART, GIZZARD, AND NECK MEAT from the **Turkey Stock for Gravy** (page 78), finely minced

¼ cup **INSTANT FLOUR** such as Wondra or Shake & Blend

3 cups **Turkey Stock for Gravy** (page 78)

KOSHER OR SEA SALT

Freshly ground **PEPPER**

In a 2½-quart saucepan over medium heat, melt the butter and swirl to coat the pan. Add the minced heart, gizzard, and neck meat and sauté until heated through, about 1 minute.

Meanwhile, in a small bowl or measuring cup, whisk together the flour and ½ cup of the stock until the flour is dissolved.

Add the remaining 2½ cups stock to the pan and bring to a simmer. Whisk in the flour mixture and simmer until the gravy thickens, about 5 minutes. Season to taste with salt and pepper. Keep warm until ready to serve.

DO AHEAD The gravy can be made up to 1 day in advance. Cover and refrigerate. Reheat gently just before serving.

Roast Turkey with Vidalia Cream Gravy

SERVES 12 TO 20, DEPENDING ON THE SIZE OF THE TURKEY

My husband had never been a fan of white turkey meat until he tasted this gravy. I couldn't believe my eyes when I saw him take a second slice of breast meat. He commented on how the naturally sweet, creamy gravy was a perfect match for the less gamey taste of the white meat. I completely agree. I'm certain I saw him take thirds and pour on more gravy when he thought I wasn't looking—it's Thanksgiving after all. It makes perfect sense to bake a batch of **Southern-Style Biscuits** (page 132) for this Thanksgiving turkey and gravy. Biscuit lovers like my husband can then drizzle gravy over the turkey as well as the biscuits.

1 large **YELLOW ONION**, chopped

1 large **CARROT**, peeled and chopped

1 large rib **CELERY**, chopped

7 **FRESH SAGE LEAVES**, chopped

1 tablespoon **FRESH THYME LEAVES**

Freshly ground **PEPPER**

One 12- to 16-pound **BRINED TURKEY** (see pages 72–73) made with **Honey and Allspice Brine** (page 77)

½ cup (1 stick) **UNSALTED BUTTER**, melted

Vidalia Cream Gravy (page 101)

In a medium bowl, combine the onion, carrot, celery, sage, thyme, and a few grinds of pepper. Mix well and set aside.

Position a rack on the second-lowest level in the oven and preheat to 500°F. Have ready a large roasting pan with a roasting rack, preferably V-shaped, set in the pan.

Put ½ cup of the vegetable mixture inside the neck cavity and ½ cup inside the chest cavity of the turkey. Scatter the remainder on the bottom of the roasting pan and add 1 cup of water to the pan. Truss the turkey, following the directions for trussing an unstuffed turkey on page 79. Using a pastry brush, brush the turkey with half of the melted butter. Place the turkey, breast side down, on the roasting rack. Roast for 30 minutes, then reduce the oven temperature to 350°F. Baste the turkey with the pan juices and roast for 30 minutes longer.

●● CONTINUED ●●

Remove the turkey from the oven. Using silicone oven mitts, regular oven mitts covered with aluminum foil, or wads of paper towels, turn the turkey breast side up. (It won't be very hot at this point.) Baste with the pan juices and the remaining melted butter, and return the turkey to the oven. Continue to roast, basting with the pan juices again after 45 minutes. At this point, check the internal temperature of the turkey by inserting an instant-read thermometer into the thickest part of a thigh without touching bone. (As a point of reference, when the internal temperature of the turkey reaches 125°F, the turkey is about 1 hour away from being done. Of course, roasting times will vary, depending on the size of the bird, its temperature when it went into the oven, whether or not it is stuffed, and your particular oven and the accuracy of the thermostat. See the chart on page 80 for guidance.) The turkey is done when the instant-read thermometer registers between 160° to 165°F when inserted into the thickest part of the thigh away from the bone.

When the turkey is done, tilt the body so the juices from the main cavity run into the pan. Transfer to a carving board or serving platter and cover loosely with aluminum foil. Let the turkey rest for 30 to 40 minutes before carving, to allow the juices to redistribute. (The internal temperature will rise 5 to 10 degrees while the turkey rests.)

Strain the juices, vegetables, and browned bits from the roasting pan through a fine-mesh sieve set over a large glass measuring cup. Set aside and allow the fat to rise to the top. Spoon off the fat. The pan juices from a brined turkey are usually too salty to add to gravy, so I refrigerate them and add to the water for making stock from the carcass; the juices provide additional flavor and the salt is diluted by the water. See After-Thanksgiving Turkey Stock, page 190.

Carve the turkey, following the directions on page 80. Serve, accompanied by the Vidalia Cream Gravy.

Vidalia Cream Gravy

MAKES ABOUT 3½ CUPS

This creamy, sweet onion gravy reminds me of the pan gravy often served with fried chicken and biscuits—but a bit more refined.

4 tablespoons (½ stick) **UNSALTED BUTTER**

1 **VIDALIA OR OTHER SWEET ONION**, finely minced

¼ cup **INSTANT FLOUR** such as Wondra or Shake & Blend

2½ cups **Turkey Stock for Gravy** (page 78)

½ cup **HEAVY (WHIPPING) CREAM**

KOSHER OR SEA SALT

Freshly ground **WHITE PEPPER**

In a 2½-quart saucepan over medium heat, melt the butter and swirl to coat the pan. Add the onion, cover, and cook until soft but not browned, about 5 minutes.

Meanwhile, in a small bowl or measuring cup, whisk together the flour and ½ cup of the stock and stir until the flour is dissolved.

Raise the heat to medium-high, add the remaining 2 cups stock and the cream to the pan with the onions, and bring to a simmer. Whisk in the flour mixture and simmer until the gravy thickens, about 5 minutes. Season to taste with salt and pepper. Keep warm until ready to serve.

DO AHEAD

The gravy can be made up to 1 day in advance. Cover and refrigerate. Reheat gently just before serving.

Roast Turkey Breast for a Small Gathering

SERVES 6

Roasting a turkey breast is a practical solution for a small Thanksgiving gathering. It's quick, makes a lovely presentation, and there will be a manageable amount of leftovers. If the die-hard, dark-meat lovers grumble, just offer them an extra piece of pie. This turkey breast will be moist, beautifully browned, and brightly flavored with lemon juice and fresh herbs.

1 whole (double) **BONE-IN TURKEY BREAST** (4½ to 5 pounds)

¼ cup **FRESH LEMON JUICE**

½ cup **EXTRA-VIRGIN OLIVE OIL**

3 tablespoons minced **FRESH ROSEMARY**

1½ tablespoons minced **FRESH THYME**

2 teaspoons minced **FRESH SAGE**

KOSHER SALT

Freshly ground **PEPPER**

1 tablespoon **ALL-PURPOSE FLOUR**

1 cup **HOMEMADE CHICKEN STOCK** (see page 11) **OR CANNED LOW-SODIUM CHICKEN BROTH**

Position a rack on the second-lowest level in the oven and preheat to 375°F. Trim any visible fat from the turkey breast, and save the neck, if included, for making gravy. Pat the turkey breast dry with paper towels. Place a rack in a roasting pan and set the turkey breast on the rack.

In a 2-cup glass measure, combine the lemon juice, olive oil, rosemary, and thyme. At the top of the breast, slide your fingers back and forth under the skin to separate it from the breast meat, creating a pocket over the entire breast. Pour half the mixture inside this pocket, and the rest over the turkey breast, coating it well. Season the turkey with salt and pepper to taste. Set the turkey breast on the rack, skin side up.

Roast the turkey breast, basting every 30 minutes, until the juices run clear when a sharp knife is inserted into the thickest part of the breast, or when an instant-read thermometer, inserted in the same spot and not touching bone, registers 165°F, about 1¼ to 1½ hours. Transfer the turkey breast to a carving board, and cover the breast loosely with aluminum foil. Allow the turkey breast to rest for 10 to 15 minutes before carving to let the juices set.

While the turkey is resting, make a quick gravy. In a small jar with a tight-fitting lid, mix together the flour and 2 tablespoons of the chicken stock. Place the roasting pan over medium heat, add the remaining stock to the pan, and bring to a simmer. Using a wooden spoon, scrape and loosen any brown bits sticking to the bottom and sides of the pan. Shake the flour mixture again and add to the stock in the pan. Stir until the gravy is smooth and thickened. Transfer to a warmed gravy boat or bowl.

Carve the turkey breast following the directions on page 80. Serve, accompanied by the gravy.

Buttermilk Brined
Roast Turkey

**SERVES 12 TO 20, DEPENDING ON
THE SIZE OF THE TURKEY**

When we think of marinating poultry in buttermilk, we think of the traditions of the American South with Sunday dinners of fried chicken. Chicken parts are bathed in buttermilk for several hours to add flavor and tenderness, and then drained and rolled in flour before pan frying it. Adapting this technique to a whole turkey, this recipe involves first rubbing a whole turkey, inside and out, with a cumin- and fennel-infused spice rub, then brining the turkey in a dilute salt solution mixed with buttermilk. After about twenty hours of brining, the turkey is rinsed, patted dry, rubbed with butter and roasted. This results in meltingly tender meat accented with the subtle tang of buttermilk and spices—a unique and glorious Thanksgiving bird for your guests.

Spice Rub

1½ teaspoons **FENNEL SEEDS**

1½ teaspoons **CUMIN SEEDS**

1 tablespoon **DRIED THYME**

1½ teaspoons coarsely ground **PEPPER**

1½ teaspoons ground **PAPRIKA**

½ teaspoon freshly grated **NUTMEG**

½ cup (2.25 ounces or 63.5 grams) **DIAMOND CRYSTAL BRAND KOSHER SALT** (see headnote, page 74)

2 cups **HOT WATER**

8 cups (2 quarts) **BUTTERMILK**

Twenty four hours prior to roasting the bird prepare the spice rub, buttermilk brine, and brine the turkey.

To make the spice rub, place the fennel and cumin seeds in small, heavy skillet over medium-high heat and toast the spices until fragrant and browned. Transfer to a spice grinder or mortar and pestle (see Cook's Note, page 75). Grind the spices to form a powder. Add the thyme, paprika, pepper, and nutmeg and mix to combine. Transfer to a small bowl and set aside.

To make the buttermilk brine, in a large bowl dissolve the salt in 2 cups of hot water. Add the buttermilk and stir to combine. Set aside.

Using the plastic oven bags, nest 1 plastic oven bag inside the other to create a double thickness. Place the double bag, mouth open wide and facing up, in the roasting pan. Fold back the top one-third of the double bag to make a collar (this helps keep the bags open). Set aside.

One 12- to 18-pound **FRESH
OR THAWED FROZEN TURKEY**
(see page 69)

1 **YELLOW ONION**, quartered

4 sprigs **FRESH THYME**

6 large **SAGE LEAVES**

6 tablespoons (¾ stick) **UNSALTED
BUTTER**, melted

Freshly ground **PEPPER**

1½ cups **HOMEMADE CHICKEN STOCK**
(see page 11) **OR CANNED LOW-
SODIUM CHICKEN BROTH**

Giblet Gravy (page 98)

Special Equipment

2 **TURKEY-SIZE PLASTIC OVEN BAGS
OR BRINING BAGS** (see Cook's Note,
page 73)

Place the turkey, still in its original wrappings, in a clean sink. Carefully slit open the plastic wrapper and remove the turkey. Remove the neck and bag of giblets from both the main cavity and neck cavity of the bird. Store them in a covered container in the refrigerator for making the gravy. Remove the plastic or metal clip holding the legs together. Pull and discard any fat pockets from the neck and main cavities of the bird. Trim off the tail, if desired, and store along with the neck and giblets for stock.

Transfer the turkey to a clean, dry work surface. Rub the bird all over with the spice rub, including inside the neck and chest cavities. Place the turkey inside the double bag. Unfold the collar of the double bag and gently pour the brine over the bird. Draw up the top of the inner bag, squeezing out as much air as possible, and secure it closed with a twist tie. Do the same with the outer bag. Turn the package so the turkey is breast side down in the roasting pan and refrigerate for at least 16 or up to 24 hours. Turn the turkey 3 or 4 times while it is brining.

Two hours prior to roasting the bird, remove the turkey from the brine. Discard the bags and brine. Rinse the turkey under cold water and pat thoroughly dry with paper towels. Place the onion, thyme, and sage inside the chest cavity of the turkey. Truss the turkey, following the directions for trussing an unstuffed turkey on page 79. Using a pastry brush, brush the turkey with the melted butter. Season the turkey with a few grinds of freshly ground pepper. Place the turkey, breast side down, on a roasting rack, preferably V-shaped, set in the roasting pan. Add the chicken stock or broth to the pan. Set aside.

Forty-five minutes prior to roasting the turkey, position a rack on the second-lowest level in the oven and preheat to 500°F.

Roast the turkey for 30 minutes. Reduce the oven temperature to 350°F. Baste the turkey with the pan juices and roast for 30 minutes longer.

●● CONTINUED ●●

Remove the turkey from the oven. Using silicone oven mitts, regular oven mitts covered with aluminum foil, or wads of paper towels, turn the turkey breast side up. (It won't be very hot at this point.) Baste with the pan juices and return the turkey to the oven. Continue to roast, basting with the pan juices again after 45 minutes. At this point, check the internal temperature of the turkey by inserting an instant-read thermometer into the thickest part of a thigh without touching bone. (As a point of reference, when the internal temperature of the turkey reaches 125°F, the turkey is about 1 hour away from being done. Of course, roasting times will vary, depending on the size of the bird, its temperature when it went into the oven, whether or not it is stuffed, and your particular oven and the accuracy of the thermostat. See the chart on page 80 for guidance.) Roast until an instant-read thermometer registers 160° to 165°F when inserted into the thickest part of the thigh without touching bone. Make the Giblet Gravy while the turkey is roasting.

When the turkey is done, tilt the body so the juices from the main cavity run into the pan. Transfer the turkey to a carving board or serving platter and cover loosely with aluminum foil. Let the turkey rest for 30 to 40 minutes before carving, to allow the juices to redistribute. (The internal temperature will rise 5 to 10 degrees while the turkey rests.)

Carve the turkey, following the directions on page 80. Serve, accompanied by the Giblet Gravy.

Jack Daniel's Whiskey and Brown Sugar Crusted Ham

SERVES 10 TO 12

For many, Thanksgiving wouldn't be complete without a holiday ham sharing center stage with the Thanksgiving roast turkey. Since hams are sold fully cooked, the only task for the cook is to glaze the ham and warm it up. If you are serving a large crowd, say, 16 to 20 guests, then you might consider buying a whole ham which includes both the shank half and the butt half and weighs about 14 to 18 pounds. Otherwise, for a gathering of 10 or so, I prefer to buy a half-ham and look for the butt half or upper part of the ham because it is more tender and tastier than the shank half. Read the label on the ham or ask your butcher for a slow-dry-cured and natural-wood-smoked ham with no water added. Adding water in the curing process dilutes the natural taste of the ham.

One 7- to 9-pound **BONE-IN SMOKED HAM**, preferably the butt or upper half

24 to 30 **WHOLE CLOVES**

1½ cups firmly packed **GOLDEN BROWN SUGAR**

1½ tablespoons **DRY MUSTARD**

5 tablespoons **JACK DANIEL'S WHISKEY**, plus 1 tablespoon for the sauce (optional)

3½ cups **APPLE CIDER**

2 tablespoons **PURE MAPLE SYRUP**

Pinch of **CAYENNE PEPPER**

1 tablespoon **CORNSTARCH** mixed with 2 tablespoons water

Remove the ham from the refrigerator 2 hours before you plan to bake it so the meat can come to room temperature. Using a sharp boning knife, trim away any skin and all but ¼ inch of the external fat from the ham. Set the ham fat side up, and make parallel cuts ½ inch deep and 1½ inches apart all over the ham. Give the ham a quarter-turn and repeat to produce a cross-hatched diamond pattern. Stick a clove in the center of each of the diamonds.

In a small bowl, mix the sugar, mustard, and 5 tablespoons whiskey into a paste and rub it all over the ham. Set the ham, fat side up, on a rack in a roasting pan just large enough to hold it without crowding. Set aside loosely covered with plastic wrap until ready to bake.

About 30 minutes prior to baking the ham, position a rack in the lower third of the oven and preheat to 350°F.

Add enough apple cider to the pan to reach ¼ inch up the sides, about 2½ cups of cider. Bake the ham, uncovered, basting at least twice with the pan juices and adding the remaining apple cider as needed to maintain a ¼-inch depth, for 1¾ to 2 hours (about 15 minutes per pound) until an instant-read thermometer inserted into the center of the ham but away from the bone registers 120°F.

● ● CONTINUED ● ●

Transfer the ham to a carving board or warmed platter and cover loosely with aluminum foil. Let the ham rest for 20 minutes to allow the juices to distribute.

Meanwhile, pour the pan juices into a 4-cup heatproof measuring cup. Set aside for 5 minutes to allow the fat to rise to the top. Spoon off the fat and discard. Pour the pan juices into a small saucepan and bring to a simmer over medium-high heat. Whisk in the maple syrup and cayenne pepper. Taste the sauce. If the flavor is concentrated and tasty, whisk in half of the cornstarch mixture and cook to thicken the sauce. If the sauce still tastes thin, simmer for a few minutes to reduce the pan juices and concentrate the flavors. Taste again, and then whisk in half the cornstarch mixture to thicken the sauce. If needed, whisk in the remaining cornstarch mixture to thicken the sauce. Add the 1 tablespoon of whiskey to the sauce, if desired. Transfer the sauce to a warmed gravy boat.

Use a sharp carving knife to cut the ham into thin slices and serve immediately. Accompany the ham with the pan sauce.

Molly's Pumpkin-and-Sage Lasagna

SERVES 8 TO 10

My daughter, Molly, was a vegetarian during her teenage years, and even now mostly eats vegetarian meals but has introduced poultry and fish back into her diet. When I wrote my first Thanksgiving book in 2001, I included an entire chapter of vegetarian entrées because so many of us cooking Thanksgiving dinner have vegetarians at the table, and we want them to eat as heartily as those of us devouring turkey with all the trimmings. I developed this pumpkin lasagna recipe for Molly, and it has remained a family favorite.

Yes, this recipe contains a long list of ingredients and has lots of directions, and, indeed, there are several steps involved in making this lasagna (see the Cook's Note for a terrific timesaving suggestion), but trust me—every bite is worth it. The combination of sautéed pumpkin sprinkled with crisp bits of fried sage leaves, layered and baked between sheets of pasta, and covered with a creamy herb-infused béchamel sauce, makes a splendid Thanksgiving entrée for your vegetarian guests. Once the various components are prepared, assembly is easy and, best of all, the lasagna can be made a day in advance, refrigerated, and then baked fresh for serving.

1 **BAY LEAF**

6 **BLACK PEPPERCORNS**

2 sprigs **FRESH THYME**

2 sprigs **FRESH PARSLEY**

3 cups **WHOLE MILK**

1 tablespoon plus 1 teaspoon **KOSHER OR SEA SALT**, plus kosher salt for sprinkling

1 pound **DRIED LASAGNA NOODLES** (1 box, or about 19 strips; see Cook's Note)

Cut an 8-inch square of cheesecloth and place the bay leaf, peppercorns, thyme, and parsley in the center. Bring up the ends to form a bag and tie securely with kitchen twine. In a 2½-quart saucepan over medium-low heat, combine the milk and bag of spices and heat until hot, but do not let the milk boil. Simmer for 2 minutes, then remove the pan from heat and let steep while you prepare the remaining ingredients.

Fill a stockpot two-thirds full of water, cover, and bring to a boil over high heat. Stir in the 1 tablespoon salt, then add the lasagna noodles, stir, and cook until al dente (cooked through, but still slightly chewy), about 10 minutes. Drain in a colander, rinse with cold water, drain again, and reserve until ready to assemble the lasagna.

●● CONTINUED ●●

●● CONTINUED ●●

¾ cup **CANOLA OIL**

½ cup **FRESH SAGE LEAVES**

2 pounds **SUGAR PUMPKIN OR BUTTER-NUT SQUASH**, peeled, halved lengthwise, seeded, and thinly sliced

¼ teaspoon **CAYENNE PEPPER**

Freshly ground **PEPPER**

1 pound **PART-SKIM RICOTTA CHEESE**

½ cup minced **FRESH FLAT-LEAF PARSLEY**

3 tablespoons **UNSALTED BUTTER**

1 large clove **GARLIC**, minced

1 small **YELLOW ONION**, thinly sliced

3 tablespoons **ALL-PURPOSE FLOUR**

¼ teaspoon freshly grated **NUTMEG**

VEGETABLE-OIL COOKING SPRAY

1 cup (4 ounces) freshly grated **PARMESAN CHEESE**, preferably Parmigiano-Reggiano

In a heavy, 8-inch sauté pan, heat the oil until it registers 365°F on a deep-frying thermometer. It should be hot, but not smoking. Have ready a baking sheet lined with a double thickness of paper towels. Working quickly, fry one-third of the sage leaves for about 5 seconds; then, using a slotted spoon, transfer to the paper towels. Fry the remaining 2 batches. Set the pan with the cooking oil aside. Generously sprinkle the sage leaves with kosher salt and set aside.

In a 12-inch sauté pan, heat 3 tablespoons of the sage-flavored oil over medium-high heat. Without crowding the pan, add slices of pumpkin and sauté until just beginning to brown, about 2 minutes. Flip the slices, sauté on the other side, and then transfer to a baking sheet lined with paper towels to drain. Repeat to cook the remaining pumpkin slices in batches, adding more flavored oil to the pan as needed. Sprinkle the sautéed pumpkin with the cayenne and black pepper to taste. Set aside.

In a medium bowl, mix together the ricotta and minced parsley. Set aside.

To make the white sauce, in a 3-quart saucepan, melt the butter over medium heat. Swirl to coat the pan, then add the garlic and onion and sauté, stirring constantly, until just beginning to brown, about 2 minutes. Add the flour to the pan and cook, stirring constantly, until the flour is blended and cooked through, about 1 minute longer. Remove the spice bag from the milk and discard. Slowly whisk the infused milk into the flour mixture, about 1 cup at a time. Bring the sauce to a simmer and cook, whisking constantly, until thick enough to coat the back of a spoon, about 5 minutes. Add the 1 teaspoon salt and the nutmeg. Stir to blend, and taste and adjust the seasoning. Set aside.

Preheat the oven to 350°F. Coat a 9-by-13-inch baking pan with cooking spray. Lay 3 strips of lasagna noodles lengthwise across the bottom of the prepared dish. Add half of the white sauce and spread evenly. Place 3 more strips of pasta in the pan. Layer half of the pumpkin slices evenly over the noodles. Crumble the fried sage leaves and sprinkle half evenly over the top. Place 3 more strips of noodles on top. Use a rubber spatula to spread all the ricotta evenly over the pasta, and then add 3 more strips of noodles. Layer the remaining pumpkin slices over the top and sprinkle with the remaining sage. Add 3 more strips of pasta, and then spread the remaining white sauce evenly on top. For the final layer, add 4 strips of noodles and sprinkle evenly with the cheese. Bake until bubbly hot and nicely browned at the edges, about 1 hour. Let rest for 10 minutes before cutting the lasagna into squares and serving.

COOK'S NOTE The recipe directions suggest boiling the lasagna noodles, which is the standard method for making lasagna. However, there are a couple of alternatives worth considering. If a pasta store in your area carries sheets of fresh pasta, substitute 6 sheets (about 1½ pounds) for the dried lasagna noodles. Lightly rinse off any flour coating the sheets, and use them without precooking. Or, buy the oven-ready, no-boil lasagna noodles available in most supermarkets, which are also time-savers. Honestly, they are a terrific product, and it's one less pot to wash. Press the top layer of the no-boil noodles into the white sauce so it gets a bit coated with sauce. Cover the lasagna with foil for the first 30 minutes of baking in order to "steam-cook" this layer; then uncover so it browns nicely.

DO AHEAD The lasagna can be assembled up to 1 day in advance. Cover and refrigerate. Bring to room temperature 1 hour before baking.

4

Stuffings, Casseroles, Biscuits, and Breads

It might be called stuffing by some and dressing by others, but everyone agrees that it's a requisite mainstay of the Thanksgiving meal. Whether baked inside the bird or prepared separately, stuffing is the ultimate comfort food, along with baked casseroles and hot-from-the oven biscuits and breads. These accompaniments are an easy way to introduce regional accents to your table, so be a culinary linguist with New England Bread Stuffing with Bell's Seasoning, Minnesota Wild Rice Dressing with Dried Fruits, and Hazelnut and Fresh Herb Popovers.

Sourdough Stuffing with Roasted Chestnuts and Apples

SERVES 12 Whether you make this as stuffing and fill the cavity of the turkey before roasting or do as I do and bake it separately as dressing, the combination of toasted sourdough bread cubes with tart apples, richly flavored roasted chestnuts, and savory sautéed vegetables and herbs makes this a sensational accompaniment to the holiday bird. Pair this with the **Juniper-Brined Roast Turkey** on page 82 or the delectable **Hickory Grill-Roasted Turkey** on page 90.

One 1-pound loaf **SOURDOUGH BREAD**, crusts removed, bread cut into ½-inch cubes

1½ pounds **FRESH CHESTNUTS** (see Cook's Note and Do Ahead)

5 tablespoons **UNSALTED BUTTER** at room temperature

1 large **YELLOW ONION**, chopped

2 large **CARROTS**, peeled and chopped

2 large ribs **CELERY**, chopped

2 **GRANNY SMITH APPLES** (about ¾ pound total weight), peeled, cored, and cut into ½-inch dice

½ cup minced **FRESH FLAT-LEAF PARSLEY**

1 tablespoon **FRESH THYME LEAVES**

1 tablespoon minced **FRESH SAGE**

1 teaspoon **KOSHER OR SEA SALT**

Freshly ground **PEPPER**

3 large **EGGS**, lightly beaten

4 cups **HOMEMADE CHICKEN STOCK** (see page 11) **OR CANNED LOW-SODIUM CHICKEN BROTH**

Preheat the oven to 400°F. Spread the bread cubes in a single layer on 2 rimmed baking sheets. Toast in the oven for 8 to 10 minutes until lightly browned. Set aside to cool. Reduce the oven temperature to 375°F.

To prepare the chestnuts, using a sharp paring knife, make a long slash on the flat side of each chestnut, cutting through the outer shell and inner brown skin. Spread the chestnuts in a single layer on a rimmed baking sheet and roast until tender when pierced with a fork, about 1 hour. Every 15 minutes, sprinkle the chestnuts with a little water. Peel the chestnuts while they are still quite warm but cool enough to handle. Using the paring knife, remove the outer shells and the inner brown skins. Discard any chestnuts that look rotten. Set aside any chestnuts that are hard to peel, then rewarm them in the 375°F oven for 2 to 3 minutes or place them on a paper towel and microwave on high for 45 seconds. Repeat as needed until easy to peel. You should have about 2 cups peeled nuts. Break all the chestnut meats into small chunks and set aside. Reduce the oven temperature to 350°F.

● ● CONTINUED ● ●

Coat a deep, 9-by-13-inch baking pan with 1 tablespoon of the butter. Place the bread cubes and chestnuts in a very large bowl. In large sauté pan, melt the remaining 4 tablespoons of butter over medium-high heat. Swirl to coat the pan and add the onion, carrots, and celery. Sauté, stirring frequently, until the onion is soft and just beginning to brown, about 4 minutes. Add the apples and sauté for 2 minutes longer. Add the parsley, thyme, sage, salt, and a few grinds of pepper and sauté for 1 minute longer. Add the apple mixture to the bread cubes and stir to combine.

Add the eggs and stock to the bowl and mix well. Scoop the stuffing into the prepared pan and bake, uncovered, for about 1 hour until the top is lightly browned and crusty.

If you have room in your oven, bake the stuffing while the turkey is roasting. Otherwise, bake it beforehand and reheat it once the turkey is out.

COOK'S NOTE   If you prefer not to roast your own chestnuts, you can buy peeled chestnuts in vacuum-sealed packages, cans, or jars at specialty-food stores. You will need about 2 cups. Drain any liquid in which they are packed. Prepared chestnuts are usually boiled rather than roasted, resulting in a bit of flavor loss. However, placing them on a rimmed baking sheet and roasting them at 375°F for 15 minutes really improves their flavor.

DO AHEAD   The bread cubes can be prepared up to 3 days in advance. Store in an airtight container at room temperature. The fresh chestnuts can be prepared up to 2 weeks in advance and frozen in lock-top freezer bags or an airtight container. Thaw the chestnuts for 1 hour, and then roast them for 10 to 12 minutes at 400°F to refresh them. The vegetables and apples can be sautéed along with the herbs 1 day in advance. Let the mixture cool completely, place it in a covered container, and refrigerate. Remove from the refrigerator 2 hours before assembling the stuffing.

Linguiça Sausage Stuffing with Mushrooms and Caramelized Onions

SERVES 12 Our culturally diverse nation may have strong Yankee roots that defined much of what we know as the traditional Thanksgiving meal, but recognizing and incorporating other wonderful ethnic foods into our harvest feast speaks to the spirit of the holiday. I couldn't resist using Portuguese linguiça sausage in this stuffing. The smoky, zesty sausage is a great match for roast or grill-roasted turkey. Ask your local butcher or specialty-foods shop about availability, or order online from *www.gasparssausage.com*, a fourth-generation family-owned business.

5 tablespoons **UNSALTED BUTTER** at room temperature

10 cups **UNSEASONED DRIED BREAD CUBES** (see Cook's Note, page 11)

1 tablespoon **OLIVE OIL**

¾ pound **LINGUIÇA SAUSAGES**

1 pound **CREMINI MUSHROOMS**, wiped or brushed clean, stems trimmed, and quartered

1 bag (14 ounces) **FROZEN PEARL ONIONS**, thawed and blotted dry with paper towels

1 tablespoon **SUGAR**

• • CONTINUED • •

Preheat the oven to 350°F. Coat a deep, 9-by-13-inch baking pan with 1 tablespoon of the butter.

Place the bread cubes in a very large bowl. In 10-inch sauté pan, heat the olive oil over medium-high heat and swirl to coat the pan. Add the sausages and cook, turning as needed, until nicely browned on all sides. Transfer to a plate and let cool. Drain all but 3 tablespoons of fat from the pan. Add the mushrooms to the pan and sauté, stirring frequently, until lightly browned, about 4 minutes. Add to the bowl with the bread cubes.

Return the pan to medium-high heat and add 2 tablespoons of the butter. Add the onions to the pan and sauté, stirring frequently, for about 3 minutes until soft and lightly browned. Sprinkle the sugar over the onions and sauté, stirring constantly, for 3 to 5 minutes until the onions turn golden and the edges caramelize. Add to the bowl with the bread and mushrooms.

• • CONTINUED • •

Linguiça Sausage Stuffing with Mushrooms and
Caramelized Onions

2 large **CARROTS**, peeled and chopped

2 large ribs **CELERY**, chopped

½ cup minced **FRESH FLAT-LEAF PARSLEY**

1 tablespoon **FRESH THYME LEAVES**

1 tablespoon minced **FRESH SAGE**

1 teaspoon **KOSHER OR SEA SALT**

Freshly ground **PEPPER**

3 large **EGGS**, lightly beaten

4 cups **HOMEMADE CHICKEN STOCK** (see page 11) **OR CANNED LOW-SODIUM CHICKEN BROTH**

Add the remaining 2 tablespoons butter to the pan. Swirl to coat the pan and add the carrots and celery. Sauté, stirring frequently, until the vegetables are soft and lightly browned, about 5 minutes. Add the parsley, thyme, sage, salt, and a few grinds of pepper and sauté for 1 minute longer. Add the vegetable-herb mixture to the bowl and stir to combine.

Cut the sausages into ¼-inch rounds and add to the stuffing. Add the eggs and stock and mix well. Scoop the stuffing into the prepared pan and bake, uncovered, for about 1 hour until the top is lightly browned and crusty.

If you have room in your oven, bake the stuffing while the turkey is roasting. Otherwise, bake it beforehand and reheat it once the turkey is out.

DO AHEAD The bread cubes can be prepared up to 3 days in advance. Store in an airtight container at room temperature. The sausages can be browned up to 1 day in advance; let cool, place in a covered container, and refrigerate. The mushrooms, onions, and vegetables can be sautéed along with the herbs up to 1 day in advance. Let the mixture cool completely and refrigerate in a covered container. Remove the sausages and vegetables from the refrigerator 2 hours before assembling the stuffing.

New England Bread Stuffing with Bell's Seasoning

SERVES 12

For New Englanders, reaching in the cupboard for Bell's Seasoning, in the bright yellow box with the blue turkey on the front, is synonymous with making stuffing. This natural, salt-free spice mixture was created by William G. Bell of Newton, Massachusetts, in 1867. It's an aromatic and herbaceous blend of rosemary, oregano, sage, ginger, marjoram, thyme, and pepper. I order Bell's online directly from the manufacturer at *www.bradyenterprises.com*.

5 tablespoons **UNSALTED BUTTER** at room temperature

9 cups **UNSEASONED DRIED BREAD CUBES** (see Cook's Note, page 11)

1 large **YELLOW ONION**, chopped

2 large **CARROTS**, peeled and chopped

2 large ribs **CELERY**, chopped

¾ cup **FRESH CRANBERRIES**, picked over and stems removed

½ cup minced **FRESH FLAT-LEAF PARSLEY**

1 tablespoon **BELL'S SEASONING**

1 teaspoon **KOSHER OR SEA SALT**

½ teaspoon freshly ground **PEPPER**

3 large **EGGS**, lightly beaten

3 cups **HOMEMADE CHICKEN STOCK** (see page 11) **OR CANNED LOW-SODIUM CHICKEN BROTH**

Preheat the oven to 350°F. Coat a deep, 9-by-13-inch baking pan with 1 tablespoon of the butter.

Place the bread cubes in a very large bowl. In a 10-inch sauté pan, melt the remaining 4 tablespoons butter over medium-high heat and swirl to coat the pan. Add the onion, carrots, and celery and sauté, stirring frequently, for about 5 minutes until the onion is soft and lightly browned. Add the onion mixture along with the cranberries to the bowl with the bread cubes and stir to combine. Using a rubber spatula, mix in the parsley, Bell's seasoning, salt, and pepper. Add the eggs and stock to the bowl and mix well. Scrape the stuffing into the prepared pan and bake, uncovered, for 45 to 50 minutes until the top is lightly browned and crusty.

If you have room in your oven, bake the stuffing while the turkey is roasting. Otherwise, bake it beforehand and reheat it once the turkey is out.

DO AHEAD

The bread cubes can be prepared up to 3 days in advance. Store in an airtight container at room temperature. The onions, celery, and carrots can be sautéed up to 1 day in advance. Let the mixture cool, place it in a covered container, and refrigerate. Remove the vegetables from the refrigerator 2 hours before assembling the stuffing.

Southern Corn Bread and Oyster Dressing

SERVES 12

I wish my father were still alive so I could make him this dressing—ah, he would love it. He grew up in Savannah, Georgia, and taught us to love Southern foods. Growing up in Pittsburgh, Pennsylvania, we would take car trips in the summer for family vacations. Many years we headed south, touring North and South Carolina, but especially Savannah. He taught me to love corn bread, oysters, crab, grits, and biscuits and gravy. This dressing is just too damn good to pass up. My dad would have had seconds.

VEGETABLE OIL COOKING SPRAY

8 cups crumbled **Corn Bread** (page 125)

5 cups **UNSEASONED DRIED BREAD CUBES** (see Cook's Note, page 11)

6 strips **BACON**, cut into 1-inch pieces

2 **YELLOW ONIONS**, cut into ½-inch dice

4 ribs **CELERY**, trimmed and cut into ½-inch dice (about 1½ cups)

1 tablespoon minced **FRESH SAGE**

1 tablespoon minced **FRESH THYME**

¼ cup minced **FRESH FLAT-LEAF PARSLEY**

1 teaspoon **FRESHLY GROUND PEPPER**

1½ pints (about 30) small **SHUCKED OYSTERS** and their liquor (see page 12)

3 large **EGGS**, lightly beaten

Preheat the oven to 350°F. Coat a deep, 9-by-13-inch baking pan with the cooking spray.

In a very large bowl, combine the corn bread and bread cubes. In a 12-inch sauté pan over medium heat, cook the bacon until crisp. Transfer to paper towels to drain, then add to the bowl with the breads. Drain all but 3 tablespoons of bacon fat from the pan, reserving any extra for another use. Place the pan over medium-low heat, add the onions and celery, and sauté, stirring frequently, for about 10 minutes until the onions are soft and but not browned. Add the sage, thyme, parsley, and pepper and sauté for 1 minute longer. Add to the bowl.

Drain the oysters through a fine-mesh sieve placed over a small bowl to catch the oyster liquor. Reserve the liquor; you should have about 1 cup. Gently stir the oysters into the bread mixture.

● ● CONTINUED ● ●

Add the eggs and oyster liquor to the bowl and mix well. Scoop the dressing into the prepared pan and bake, uncovered, for about 1 hour until the top is lightly browned and crusty.

If you have room in your oven, bake the stuffing while the turkey is roasting. Otherwise, bake it beforehand and reheat it once the turkey is out.

DO AHEAD   The corn bread can be prepared up to 1 day in advance. Store in an airtight container at room temperature. The bread cubes can be prepared up to 3 days in advance. Store in an airtight container at room temperature. Once assembled, the dressing can be covered and refrigerated for up to 6 hours. Bring to room temperature before baking.

Corn Bread

MAKES ONE 9-BY-13-INCH
CORN BREAD; ENOUGH FOR
8 CUPS CRUMBLED,
PLUS EXTRA FOR SNACKING

This is quick to assemble, quick to bake, and beats any store-bought or made-from-a-mix corn bread.

VEGETABLE OIL COOKING SPRAY

2 cups MEDIUM-GRIND
YELLOW CORNMEAL

½ cup ALL-PURPOSE FLOUR

1 teaspoon KOSHER OR SEA SALT

1 tablespoon SUGAR

2 teaspoons BAKING SODA

1 can (15 ounces) CREAMED CORN

1 cup BUTTERMILK

4 large EGGS, lightly beaten

¾ cup (1½ sticks) UNSALTED BUTTER,
melted

Preheat the oven to 375°F. Coat a 9-by-13-inch baking pan with the cooking spray.

In a large bowl, whisk together the cornmeal, flour, salt, sugar, and baking soda. Add the corn, buttermilk, and eggs, stirring just to blend. Stir in the butter just until combined. Pour the batter into the prepared pan and smooth the top with a rubber spatula.

Bake for about 45 minutes until the corn bread is golden brown and a toothpick inserted into the center comes out clean. Let cool in the pan for 15 minutes, then turn out onto a wire rack to cool completely.

Pan-Asian Rice Dressing

SERVES 10 TO 12 The unique foods of Thanksgiving aren't part of the traditional Asian diet. To bridge this gap, I researched recipes and found delicious stuffings that use rice, ginger, chestnuts, and even Chinese sausage. On Thanksgiving, many Asian American families serve roasted duck instead of turkey. The essential spirit of the holiday is inclusiveness, regardless of foods served.

3 cups **LONG-GRAIN RICE**

1½ cups **DRIED BLACK OR SHIITAKE MUSHROOMS** (about 18)

2 tablespoons **PEANUT OIL**

3 cloves **GARLIC**, minced

2 tablespoons finely minced **FRESH GINGER**

2 **CARROTS**, trimmed, peeled, and cut on the diagonal into ⅛-inch-thick slices

1 pound **FRESH WATER CHESTNUTS**, peeled and sliced, or 2 cans (8 ounces each) sliced water chestnuts, drained (see Cook's Notes)

12 ounces **CHINESE PORK SAUSAGE**, cut on the diagonal into ¼-inch-thick slices (see Cook's Notes)

COOKED GIBLETS from 1 turkey, diced (optional)

3 tablespoons **SOY SAUCE**

2 tablespoons **ASIAN SESAME OIL**

½ cup thinly sliced **GREEN ONIONS**, including tender green tops

Place the rice in a bowl and cover with cold water. Swish the rice, washing it in several changes of cold water until the water runs clear. This removes the residual starch. Drain in a sieve. Place the rice in a heavy 3-quart saucepan and add 3½ cups water. Cover the pan and bring the water to a boil over high heat, about 5 minutes. Reduce the heat to low and cook the rice at a bare simmer for 15 minutes. As tempting as it might be, don't remove the lid and peek at any point, or all the steam will escape. Remove from the heat and let stand for 10 minutes. Fluff with a fork and spread out on a rimmed baking sheet to dry a bit. (Alternatively, use a rice cooker and follow the manufacturer's instructions.)

Meanwhile, place the mushrooms in a bowl and add just enough hot water to cover the mushrooms by 1 inch. Place a piece of plastic wrap directly on top of the water to help keep the mushrooms submerged. Soak the mushrooms for about 20 minutes until softened. Drain the mushrooms through a fine-mesh sieve set over a small bowl to catch the mushroom soaking liquid. Reserve ½ cup of the liquid. Trim and discard the mushroom stems and cut the caps into thin slices. Set aside.

●● CONTINUED ●●

Place a 14-inch wok or 12-inch skillet over high heat and add the peanut oil. Swirl to coat the wok and heat the oil just until it begins to smoke. Add the garlic and ginger and stir-fry for 30 seconds. Add the carrots, water chestnuts, and sausage and stir-fry for about 3 minutes until the carrots and water chestnuts are crisp-tender and the sausages are heated through and caramelized at the edges. Add the mushrooms and turkey giblets and stir-fry for 1 minute longer. Stir in the reserved rice, mushroom liquid, soy sauce, and sesame oil. Stir-fry for about 3 minutes until the rice is hot. Add the green onions and stir-fry for 1 minute longer. Transfer to a warmed serving bowl and serve immediately, or keep warm for up to 1 hour.

COOK'S NOTES I prefer to buy fresh water chestnuts, available in Asian markets, because they have a sweet, nutty flavor and crunchy texture that is lost when they are processed and canned. That said, the fresh ones are a bit of a chore to peel and prepare. Use them if you, or a kitchen helper, has time to prepare them. Scrub them thoroughly to get off any mud clinging to the skins and use a sharp paring knife to peel them. Slice them crosswise into rounds.

Chinese pork sausage, or *laap cheong*, is a dried, hard sausage typically made from pork and pork fat that has been seasoned, sweetened, and smoked. It is sold unpackaged in Asian markets often tied in clusters and hanging above the meat counter, or it is sold in vacuum-sealed packages in the refrigerated case in Asian supermarkets.

DO AHEAD The rice dressing can be made up to 1 day in advance. Let cool, cover, and refrigerate. Remove from the refrigerator 1 hour before reheating. Reheat in a 250°F oven in a covered, oven-to-table casserole. Alternatively, the rice dressing can be transferred to a covered, microwave-safe casserole and reheated in the microwave on high.

Minnesota Wild Rice Dressing with Dried Fruits

SERVES 8 TO 10

Long considered the "caviar of grains," wild rice is native to North American, and isn't really a rice at all. The grains are long, slender, and black, with a unique nutty, almost smoky, flavor. They come from a reed-like aquatic plant that not long ago was only found in the wild, but is now naturally cultivated. Local Indians still gather wild rice by paddling in canoes through the rice beds of Minnesota. Wild rice also grows in the southern states of the United States as well as rural mountain valleys of Northern California. Wild rice pairs beautifully with game birds, chicken, and a holiday turkey. I like to serve this separately, but it is equally delicious stuffed in the bird.

2 cups wild **RICE**

2 cups **HOMEMADE CHICKEN STOCK** (see page 11) **OR CANNED LOW-SODIUM CHICKEN BROTH**

½ teaspoon **KOSHER OR SEA SALT**

½ cup **PINE NUTS**

¾ cup dried **APRICOTS**, quartered

5 tablespoons unsalted **BUTTER**

2 large ribs **CELERY**, finely chopped

2 large **CARROTS**, peeled and finely chopped

1 yellow **ONION**, finely chopped

1 tablespoon **FRESH THYME LEAVES**

1 tablespoon minced **FRESH SAGE**

½ cup minced **FRESH FLAT-LEAF PARSLEY**

½ cup sweetened dried **CRANBERRIES**

Freshly ground **PEPPER**

In a medium saucepan, combine the rice, stock, 1/4 teaspoon of the salt, and 2 cups water. Bring to a boil over medium-high heat. Reduce the heat to a simmer, cover partially, and cook, stirring occasionally, until the rice is tender, about 40 minutes. (Not all of the liquid will be absorbed.)

Meanwhile, place a small, heavy skillet over medium-high heat. When it is hot, but not smoking, add the pine nuts. Stirring constantly, toast them until nicely browned, about 3 to 5 minutes. Transfer to a plate and set aside to cool.

Place the dried apricots in a small bowl, add hot water to cover, and allow to plump for 20 minutes. Drain and set aside.

In a 10-inch sauté pan over medium-high heat, melt 4 tablespoons of the butter. Swirl to coat the pan, add the celery, carrot, and onion, and sauté until the onion is soft and lightly browned, about 5 minutes. Add the thyme, sage, and parsley and sauté for 1 minute longer. Remove from the heat.

Preheat the oven to 350°F. When the rice is tender, stir in the sautéed vegetable mixture. Add the toasted pine nuts, plumped apricots, and dried cranberries. Stir to combine. Add the remaining 1/4 teaspoon salt and a few grinds of pepper. Taste and adjust the seasoning.

•• CONTINUED ••

Use the remaining 1 tablespoon butter to grease an oven-to-table casserole dish. Spoon the rice mixture into the prepared pan and cover. Shortly before serving, bake the wild rice until heated through, about 20 minutes.

DO AHEAD   The dressing can be made up to 1 day in advance. Cover and refrigerate. Bring to room temperature 1 hour before baking. Increase the baking time to 40 minutes to ensure that the stuffing is heated through.

Southern-Style Biscuits

MAKES ABOUT 15 BISCUITS

The lightest, loftiest, and most tender biscuits are always made with Southern flour, such as White Lily or Martha White brands, which are milled from soft wheat flour. Though this flour is readily available in the Southern states and Texas, it is harder to obtain in other regions of the country. I order mine online from *www.smuckers.com*. An alternative, though not quite as good, is to substitute 2 cups of self-rising all-purpose flour and increase the baking soda to 1 teaspoon.

I need to thank Leslie Cole, staff writer at the *Oregonian*, for a timely "FOODday" article on pie crusts. She discussed leaf lard, a high-quality lard rendered from the prime pork fat called leaf fat. She writes, "It's creamy, mild, and a far cry from the greasy blocks of commercial lard sold at supermarkets, which are partially hydrogenated, highly processed, and not what you want in your pie-making bag of tricks." It's not what you want in your biscuits, either. Call your local butcher shop and ask for leaf lard. It's more readily available then I realized, and worth the extra effort.

VEGETABLE OIL COOKING SPRAY

2 cups **SOUTHERN SELF-RISING FLOUR**

½ tablespoon **SUGAR**

¼ teaspoon **BAKING SODA**

¼ teaspoon **KOSHER OR SEA SALT**

¼ cup packed ice-cold **LARD OR VEGETABLE SHORTENING**

2 tablespoons ice-cold **UNSALTED BUTTER**, diced

⅔ to ¾ cup **BUTTERMILK**

ALL-PURPOSE FLOUR for dusting (see Cook's Note)

Preheat the oven to 475°F. Spray a rimmed baking sheet or 9-inch round cake pan with the cooking spray.

For light biscuits, spoon the flour into a measuring cup and sweep the back of a table knife across the top to level the flour and get an accurate measure. Place the flour in a large bowl. Add the sugar, baking soda, and salt and whisk to blend. Scatter the lard and butter pieces over the top. Using a pastry blender or 2 knives, cut the lard and butter into the flour until the mixture resembles coarse meal with the bits of fat about the size of small peas. Make a well in the center of the flour and add the buttermilk, stirring just to blend well.

Dust a work surface with all-purpose flour and turn the dough out onto the prepared surface. Fold and pat the dough gently to build up the layers, making 5 or 6 turns, just until the dough holds together and can be rolled out, using as little additional flour as possible to keep the dough from sticking. Using your fingertips, gently press the dough into a circle about ½ inch thick.

Using a 2½-inch, sharp-edged biscuit cutter, cut straight down without twisting the cutter to form biscuits. (If you twist the cutter the biscuits will be lopsided.) Reshape any remaining dough and cut more biscuits. Place the rounds on the prepared baking sheet, 1 inch apart for crusty-sided biscuits or almost touching for soft-sided biscuits. Bake for about 12 minutes until golden brown. Serve warm, or rewarm just before serving.

COOK'S NOTE It is important to switch from self-rising flour to all-purpose flour for shaping the biscuits because the leavener in the self-rising flour would make the outside of the biscuits taste bitter.

DO AHEAD Of course, biscuits straight from the oven are the ideal, but that gets complicated on Thanksgiving Day. Here are some do-ahead options: Make the biscuits early in the day and rewarm them just before serving. Or make the dough, cut the biscuits, place them on a baking sheet, and cover and refrigerate; then bake just before serving. Or you can also make the biscuits a couple days ahead, underbake them a bit, and freeze them. Then without thawing them, finish baking to heat them through.

Sizzlin' Corn and Jalapeño Bread with Bacon

SERVES 10 Get out your well-seasoned cast iron skillet and make a batch of this crisp-edged, big-flavored corn bread to go with the holiday bird. The secret is to get the skillet sizzlin' hot before adding the batter.

1¼ cups **BUTTERMILK**

1 cup **YELLOW MEDIUM-GRIND CORNMEAL**

5 strips **BACON**, cut into ½-inch dice

1 cup **ALL-PURPOSE FLOUR**

2 tablespoons **SUGAR**

1 teaspoon **BAKING POWDER**

¾ teaspoon **KOSHER OR SEA SALT**

½ teaspoon **BAKING SODA**

2 large **EGGS**, lightly beaten

1 can (15 ounces) **CREAMED CORN**

1 cup (4 ounces) shredded **PEPPER JACK CHEESE**

⅓ cup diced **RED BELL PEPPER**

1 to 2 **JALAPEÑO CHILES**, seeded, deribbed, and minced (see Cook's Note, page 40)

Position a rack in the center of the oven and preheat to 400°F. Have ready a 12-inch cast iron skillet with 2-inch sides.

In a large bowl, combine the buttermilk and cornmeal and stir to mix. Set aside for 30 minutes.

Meanwhile, scatter the bacon in the skillet and cook it over medium heat until crisp. Using a slotted spoon, transfer the bacon to a plate lined with paper towels to drain. Set aside. Pour all the bacon fat from the pan into a heatproof measuring cup. Reserve ¼ cup of the bacon fat and discard the rest or save it for another use. Set the skillet aside.

Sift together the flour, sugar, baking powder, salt, and baking soda into a bowl. Using a rubber spatula, fold the dry ingredients into the buttermilk mixture, folding just until the flour disappears. Add the eggs and reserved ¼ cup bacon fat, mixing gently to combine. Stir in the corn, cheese, bell peppers, and chile to taste. Place the skillet in the oven and preheat for about 5 minutes until sizzling hot. Spread the batter in the hot skillet.

Bake for about 40 to 45 minutes until the edges are crisp and dark brown and a toothpick inserted into the center comes out clean. Transfer to a wire rack. Cool for 10 minutes. Cut into wedges and serve warm.

COOK'S NOTE To achieve the desired dark, extra-crispy edges for the corn bread, it is best to bake it in a hot cast iron skillet. If you don't have a cast iron skillet, bake the corn bread in a heavy, 12-inch skillet with an ovenproof handle, or in a 2-quart rectangular baking pan.

DO AHEAD The corn bread can be baked up to 8 hours in advance. Set aside at room temperature. Reheat the corn bread in a hot oven for 10 minutes right before you are planning to serve.

Hazelnut and
Fresh Herb Popovers

MAKES 12 POPOVERS

You are probably reading this recipe and thinking—how could I possibly pull off popovers at Thanksgiving? The trick is to have the batter made, the butter melted, and the pan ready. As soon as the turkey comes out of the oven, the muffin tin gets heated and buttered, and the popovers go in. The burst of heat makes them puff and crisp—with a golden, nutty exterior and a soft, hollow interior. They're divine.

1 cup **ALL-PURPOSE FLOUR**

½ cup **HAZELNUTS**, toasted (see Cook's Note, page 60) and finely ground

¼ teaspoon freshly ground **PEPPER**

¼ teaspoon **KOSHER OR SEA SALT**

1¼ cups **MILK**

3 large **EGGS**, beaten

2 tablespoons minced **FRESH FLAT-LEAF PARSLEY**

1 tablespoon snipped **FRESH CHIVES**

5 tablespoons **UNSALTED BUTTER**, melted

In a medium bowl, or preferably a 4-cup glass measuring cup, combine the flour, hazelnuts, pepper, and salt. Slowly whisk in the milk until smooth. Whisk in the eggs and then add the parsley and chives. Whisk in 2 tablespoons of the butter. Let the batter stand at room temperature for at least 30 minutes or up to 2 hours. Whisk before using.

Position a rack in the center of the oven and preheat to 450°F. Have ready a standard 12-cup muffin pan, preferably nonstick.

Place the muffin pan in the oven for about 10 minutes until hot. Remove the hot muffin pan from the oven. Using a pastry brush, generously brush the muffin cups with the remaining 3 tablespoons butter. Divide the batter equally among the muffin cups. Without opening the oven door at any time, bake the popovers for 15 minutes. Reduce the oven to 350°F and continue to bake the popovers for 7 to 10 minutes longer until puffy and golden brown. Turn the popovers out of the pan, loosening them with the edge of a paring knife, if necessary. Serve immediately.

DO AHEAD The batter can be made up to 2 hours in advance. The popovers are best when baked right before serving.

Heartland Cottage Cheese Dill Bread

MAKES 1 ROUND LOAF

When I lived in Chicago years ago, my cooking mentor was Alma Lach. Alma had been food editor of the *Chicago Sun-Times* for twenty years before retiring and opening a prominent avocational cooking school. She learned to cook "properly," as her late husband, Donald, would say, at Le Cordon Bleu in Paris, but she grew up on a farm in downstate Illinois with wonderful canning and bread-making traditions. This is her farm-style recipe. A treasured one.

¼ cup **WARM (110°F) WATER**

2 tablespoons **SUGAR**

1 envelope (¼ ounce) **ACTIVE DRY YEAST**

3 tablespoons **UNSALTED BUTTER** at room temperature

1 cup **SMALL-CURD COTTAGE CHEESE**

1 tablespoon chopped **DRIED ONIONS**

1 tablespoon **DILL SEEDS**

1 teaspoon **DRIED DILL WEED**

1 teaspoon **DRIED ITALIAN HERB SEASONING**

1 teaspoon **DRIED BASIL**

1¼ teaspoons **KOSHER OR SEA SALT**

¼ teaspoon **BAKING SODA**

1 large **EGG**, at room temperature, beaten

2¼ cups **ALL-PURPOSE FLOUR**

In a small bowl, combine the water and ¼ teaspoon of the sugar. Sprinkle the yeast over the top. Stir to wet the yeast and set aside until foamy, about 8 minutes.

In a small saucepan over medium-low heat, melt 1 tablespoon of the butter. Add the cottage cheese and heat it to 110°F on an instant-read thermometer, stirring constantly. Remove from the heat and stir in the remaining sugar, the dried onions, dill seeds, dill weed, herb seasoning, basil, and 1 teaspoon of the salt. Transfer to a large bowl. Add the baking soda, egg, and yeast mixture. Using a wooden spoon, stir in the flour, mixing well and scraping down the sides of the bowl to incorporate all the flour. Cover the bowl with a damp, clean kitchen towel and let rise at room temperature for about 1 hour until doubled in bulk.

Punch down the dough. Generously butter a 2½-quart soufflé dish, straight-sided oven-to-table casserole, or 9-by-5-inch loaf pan with 1 tablespoon of the remaining butter. Turn the dough into the prepared dish or pan. Cover with a damp, clean kitchen towel and let rise at room temperature for about 1 hour until doubled in bulk again.

Meanwhile, position a rack in the lower third of the oven and preheat to 350°F.

Bake the bread for about 40 minutes until deeply golden brown. Immediately brush the bread with the remaining 1 tablespoon butter and sprinkle with the remaining ¼ teaspoon salt. Transfer to a wire rack and let the bread cool in the dish for 15 minutes. Using a table knife, loosen the sides of the bread from the pan, turn out onto the rack, and let cool to warm.

DO AHEAD   Bake the bread 1 day in advance. Warm before serving.

5

Festive Side Dishes

Dazzling side dishes share center stage at our holiday table, even though our colonial forefathers considered vegetables to be secondary and inferior food. With this country's renewed emphasis on local, fresh-from-the grower produce, admonishing your guests to eat their vegetables seems an artifact from a bygone era. The challenge today is to keep your hungry hordes from filling up on ambrosial—and yes, sometimes decadently rich—side dishes, such as Maple-Mashed Sweet Potatoes, Butter-Mashed Yukon Gold Potatoes with Parmesan, Roasted Carrots and Parsnips with Fresh Herbs, and Creamed Pearl Onions with Bacon.

Honey and Chipotle Glazed
Sweet Potato Spears with Lime

SERVES 10

Whether we are celebrating Thanksgiving as a Native American or as a descendent of Spanish explorers, Pilgrims, or other immigrant groups, we tend to take the traditional foods and give them our own cultural twist. This sensational and easy recipe reflects the influences of Southwestern cuisine—roasting sweet potatoes with chipotle powder, fresh lime juice, and honey.

4 pounds uniformly (medium) size **DARK-ORANGE-FLESHED SWEET POTATOES**, (see page 15) peeled, cut in half crosswise, then cut into ½-inch wedges

1 tablespoon plus ½ cup (1 stick) **UNSALTED BUTTER** at room temperature

1 teaspoon **CHIPOTLE POWDER**

½ cup **HONEY**

⅓ cup **FRESH LIME JUICE**

1 teaspoon **KOSHER OR SEA SALT**

Preheat the oven to 400°F. Place the sweet potato wedges in a large bowl. Coat a large rimmed baking sheet with the 1 tablespoon butter and set aside.

In a small saucepan over medium heat, melt the ½ cup butter. Whisk in the chipotle powder and then add the honey, lime juice, and salt. Bring to a simmer, stirring constantly; continue simmering for 3 minutes to meld the glaze.

Pour the glaze over the sweet potatoes and toss until well coated. Arrange them in a single layer on the prepared baking sheet. Use a rubber spatula to scrape the bowl, drizzling any remaining glaze over the potatoes. Cover the pan tightly with aluminum foil. Roast, covered, for 40 minutes. Remove the foil and baste the potatoes. Continue to bake, basting every 10 minutes, for about 20 minutes longer until tender, nicely browned, and caramelized at the edges. Serve immediately, or keep warm in a low oven for up to 30 minutes. Baste just before serving.

DO AHEAD

The sweet potatoes can be roasted up to 1 day in advance. Refrigerate, covered, and bring to room temperature 2 hours before reheating. Alternatively, they can be roasted up to 4 hours in advance and set aside at room temperature. Reheat before serving, basting with the glaze.

Maple-Mashed Sweet Potatoes

SERVES 10 TO 12

A gift to the early colonists from Native American cooks was the boiled-down sap of the rock maple or sugar maple. Though maple syrup is produced in other parts of the East as well as the Midwest, we primarily associate maple syrup with New England. It's the image of a farmer bundled up and trudging through the snow in late winter to tap his trees that comes to mind. This recipe couldn't be easier or more delightful.

5 pounds **DARK-ORANGE-FLESHED SWEET POTATOES**, (see page 15) scrubbed

½ cup (1 stick) **UNSALTED BUTTER**

¾ cup **PURE MAPLE SYRUP**

⅔ to ¾ cup **MILK**, warmed

KOSHER OR SEA SALT

Preheat the oven to 350°F. Pierce each potato several times with a fork and place in a baking pan. Bake the potatoes for 1¼ to 1½ hours until tender when pierced with a fork. Set aside until cool enough to handle.

In a small saucepan over medium-high heat, combine the butter and maple syrup. Stir to melt the butter and bring to a boil. Set aside and keep warm.

Cut the potatoes in half and scoop the flesh into a large bowl, discarding the skins. Use a potato masher, ricer, or food mill to mash the potatoes. Stir the butter mixture into the potatoes. Add the milk and mash until well blended. Season to taste with salt. Transfer the mashed potatoes to a saucepan and heat over medium heat for about 10 minutes until warmed through. Alternatively, transfer the mashed potatoes to a microwave-safe serving bowl and cover with plastic wrap. Just before serving, microwave the potatoes on high until heated through.

DO AHEAD

The mashed potatoes can be made up to 1 day in advance. Cover and refrigerate. Bring to room temperature 2 hours before reheating.

Butter-Mashed Yukon Gold Potatoes with Parmesan

SERVES 8

There is no such thing as too many starchy dishes on the holiday buffet table, right? For many families, Thanksgiving dinner wouldn't be complete without mashed potatoes. Deliciously different from russet potatoes, mashed Yukon golds are creamy rich with a buttery texture and a lovely golden hue. They have a higher moisture content and are lower in starch than the russet potato, and therefore require a different proportion of milk and butter when puréed. Be sure to have plenty of gravy on hand, as your guests will be ladling gravy over the potatoes as well as the stuffing.

6 large **YUKON GOLD POTATOES** (about 2½ pounds total weight)

1 teaspoon **KOSHER OR SEA SALT**, plus extra for seasoning

1 cup **MILK**

½ cup **HEAVY (WHIPPING) CREAM**

½ cup (1 stick) **UNSALTED BUTTER**, melted

⅓ cup (1½ ounces) freshly grated **PARMESAN CHEESE**, preferably Parmigiano-Reggiano

Freshly ground **PEPPER**

Peel the potatoes and rinse under cold water. Cut each into quarters and place in a 3- to 4-quart saucepan. Cover with cold water, partially cover the pot, and bring the water to a boil over high heat. Uncover, add the 1 teaspoon salt, and reduce the heat so the water boils gently. Cook for about 10 to 12 minutes until the potatoes are tender when pierced with a fork. Meanwhile, in a small saucepan, heat the milk and cream just until hot, but not boiling.

Drain the potatoes, return to the warm pan, and stir over low heat for 1 minute to evaporate any excess water. Use a potato masher, ricer, or food mill to mash the potatoes. Blend the butter and cheese into the potatoes. Stir the milk mixture into the potatoes, a little at a time, until the potatoes are as soft and moist as you like. Add salt and pepper to taste. Serve immediately.

DO AHEAD

To avoid last-minute chaos in the kitchen, know that it works perfectly well to cook and mash potatoes up to 2 hours in advance. They can be kept warm in the top of a double boiler set over simmering water, or reheated in a microwave oven just before serving. If you use the do-ahead plan, be sure to add an extra pat of butter or two.

Sweet Potato Purée
with Pecan Streusel

SERVES 10   A casserole of candied yams with marshmallow topping is traditional on many Thanksgiving tables, but I wanted to give this classic an updated twist, so I have made it with a pecan streusel topping. For years, I have taught Thanksgiving classes around the country. Every time the students sample this recipe, they tell me it is the best they have ever tasted. The sweet potatoes are lightened with eggs and enriched with butter and brown sugar—but the pecan streusel topping hot from the oven is meltingly lush and browned to a caramelized crisp.

5 pounds **DARK-ORANGE-FLESHED SWEET POTATOES,** (see page 15) scrubbed

½ cup (1 stick) plus 1 tablespoon **UNSALTED BUTTER** at room temperature

¾ cup firmly packed **DARK BROWN SUGAR**

¾ cup **MILK,** warmed

3 large **EGGS,** lightly beaten

Streusel Topping

¾ cup coarsely finely chopped **PECANS**

½ cup **ALL-PURPOSE FLOUR**

½ cup firmly packed **DARK BROWN SUGAR**

¾ teaspoon **GROUND CINNAMON**

½ teaspoon freshly grated **NUTMEG**

½ teaspoon **KOSHER OR SEA SALT**

½ cup (1 stick) **UNSALTED BUTTER,** melted

½ cup **HEAVY (WHIPPING) CREAM**

Position a rack in the center of the oven and preheat to 350°F. Pierce each potato several times with a fork and place them in a baking pan. Bake for 1¼ to 1½ hours until very tender when pierced with a fork. Set aside until cool.

In a small saucepan over medium heat, melt the ½ cup butter. Add the brown sugar and cook, stirring, until the sugar is dissolved and the mixture is bubbly hot. Set aside. Cut the potatoes in half, scoop the flesh into a large bowl, and discard the skins. Mash with a potato masher, or pass the potatoes through a ricer or food mill held over a bowl. Stir the butter mixture into the mashed potatoes. Add the milk and stir until incorporated. Whisk in the eggs until well combined.

Coat a 3-quart oval gratin dish or an 11-inch round oven-to-table casserole with the 1 tablespoon butter. Spread the sweet potato mixture evenly in the casserole. Set aside while making the topping. Raise the oven temperature to 375°F.

To make the streusel topping, in a bowl, combine the pecans, flour, sugar, cinnamon, nutmeg, and salt. Stir in the melted butter and cream. Spread the streusel topping evenly over the sweet potatoes. Bake for about 40 minutes until the potatoes are hot throughout and the topping is nicely browned and crisp. Serve immediately.

DO AHEAD   The whipped sweet potatoes and topping can be made up to 1 day in advance. Cover and refrigerate in separate containers. Remove 2 hours before baking. Warm the topping and spread it over the potatoes.

New England
Iron-Skillet Succotash

SERVES 10 TO 12   The Narragansett ate succotash of corn and beans cooked in bear fat. They called it "misickquatash." It has evolved over the years into a delicious dish, which is certainly lower in cholesterol! Served on many Thanksgiving tables, especially in New England, succotash is a colorful addition to the plate.

5 **FRESH EARS OF CORN**
(see Cook's Note)

3 tablespoons **UNSALTED BUTTER**

2 medium **ZUCCHINI**, cut into ½-inch dice

2 medium **GOLDEN ZUCCHINI**, cut into ½-inch dice

1 large **WHITE ONION**, cut into ½-inch dice

2 medium **RED BELL PEPPERS**, seeded, deribbed, and cut into ½-inch dice

1 package (10 ounces) **FROZEN LIMA BEANS**, thawed

½ cup minced **FRESH PARSLEY**

KOSHER OR SEA SALT

Freshly ground **PEPPER**

Remove the husks and silk from the ears of corn and discard. Trim the base of each ear so it is even and flat. Working with 1 ear at a time, stand it upright on its base in a bowl. Using a sharp knife, cut down between the cob and the kernels to remove the kernels. Reserve the kernels and discard the cobs.

Fill a large saucepan two-thirds full of water and bring to a boil over high heat. Add the corn and simmer for 3 minutes. Drain in a colander, then rinse under cold water until cool. Drain thoroughly, blot dry with paper towels, and set aside.

In a 12-inch skillet, preferably cast iron, melt the butter over medium-high heat and swirl to coat the pan. Add the zucchinis and onion and sauté, stirring frequently, for about 5 minutes until just beginning to brown at the edges. Add the red peppers and sauté for 3 minutes longer. Add the lima beans and corn kernels. Sauté, stirring constantly, for about 2 minutes until the vegetables are heated through. Stir in the parsley and season with salt and pepper to taste. Serve immediately, or keep warm for up to 20 minutes.

COOK'S NOTE   Nowadays, with our global markets, fresh corn is available year-round. In November, I don't buy fresh corn to eat on the cob (I save that eating pleasure for summer, when the corn is local and freshly picked). However, I do use November corn in sautés and soups—in fact, I prefer fresh corn to frozen because the texture is tender and firm. The variety of corn available in the markets at this time of year is, most likely, a hybrid known as Super-Sweet. As a result of the high sugar content, the corn caramelizes when sautéed, which gives a welcome, rich flavor to the succotash.

DO AHEAD   This sauté is best when made right before serving. However, the corn can be blanched and the vegetables can all be chopped up to 1 day in advance.

Roasted Carrots and Parsnips with Fresh Herbs

SERVES 8 TO 10

Here's one vegetable dish that doesn't need last-minute attention from the busy Thanksgiving cook—and I'm thankful for that. These orange and ivory root vegetables, flecked with fresh herbs, complement turkey and are a colorful addition to the holiday table. Parsnips are woefully underused; once most people try them, they are surprised by how sweet and pleasantly complex they taste. They will keep, wrapped in paper towels and slipped into a plastic bag, in the refrigerator for up to 2 weeks. They are also terrific combined with potatoes for a puréed winter soup, such as my recipe for **Silky Parsnip-Potato Soup Garnished with Crisp Diced Bacon** (page 47).

7 **PARSNIPS** (about 2½ pounds total weight), peeled, trimmed, and cut into 3-by-½-inch sticks

1½ pounds tender **CARROTS**, peeled, trimmed, and cut into 3-by-½-inch sticks

⅓ cup **EXTRA-VIRGIN OLIVE OIL**

1 tablespoon chopped **FRESH DILL**

1 tablespoon minced **FRESH FLAT-LEAF PARSLEY**

1 teaspoon freshly ground **PEPPER**

2 teaspoons **KOSHER OR SEA SALT**

Position a rack in the center of the oven and preheat to 400°F.

In a large roasting pan or 9-by-13-inch baking dish, toss the parsnips and carrots with the olive oil, dill, parsley, pepper, and salt. Roast, stirring once or twice, for about 45 minutes until the vegetables are tender when pierced with a knife and lightly caramelized in spots. Serve immediately, or cover and keep warm for up to 1 hour before serving.

DO AHEAD

The roasted vegetables can be made up to 1 day in advance. Refrigerate, covered, and bring to room temperature 2 hours before reheating.

Southwest Simmered Green Beans with Garlic and Onions

SERVES 10

New World flavors come together in this Southwestern sauté to accompany the holiday bird. I love to pair it with the **Hickory Grill-Roasted Turkey** on page 90 and the **Honey and Chipotle Glazed Sweet Potato Spears with Lime** on page 142.

3 tablespoons **EXTRA-VIRGIN OLIVE OIL**

2 large cloves **GARLIC**, minced

1 large **YELLOW ONION**, halved lengthwise, and cut into thin wedges

2 teaspoons **GROUND CUMIN**

1½ pounds **FRESH GREEN BEANS**, stem ends trimmed

1 can (28 ounces) **DICED TOMATOES**

½ teaspoon **RED PEPPER FLAKES**

1 teaspoon **KOSHER OR SEA SALT**

Heat the olive oil in a 14-inch skillet over medium heat and swirl to coat the pan. Add the garlic and onion and sauté, stirring frequently, for about 4 minutes until soft but not browned. Add the cumin and sauté for 2 minutes longer. Add the green beans and sauté, stirring constantly, for about 3 minutes until the beans turn bright green. Add the diced tomatoes, including the juice from the can, and stir in the red pepper flakes and salt. Reduce the heat to low, cover, and simmer for 10 to 12 minutes until the beans are crisp-tender. Serve immediately, or keep warm for up to 30 minutes.

DO AHEAD

This sauté is best when made right before serving. However, the vegetables can be prepared and chopped up to 8 hours in advance. Cover and set aside at room temperature.

Green Beans with Lemon-Butter Bread Crumbs and Toasted Almonds

SERVES 6 TO 8

If truth be told, this cookbook does not contain the classic Thanksgiving green bean bake. I'm just not a fan. My grandmother made it, my mother made it, but I've not passed that tradition to my children. I've updated the classic using fresh green beans and toasted slivered almonds, and have skipped the condensed mushroom soup in favor of a spritz of fresh lemon juice. The topping is buttery-crisp *panko* tossed with fresh lemon zest. It's a fresh-tasting winner.

5 tablespoons **UNSALTED BUTTER**

¾ cup *PANKO* (Japanese bread crumbs) or other plain dried bread crumbs

Zest of 1 **LEMON**

KOSHER OR SEA SALT

1½ pounds **FRESH GREEN BEANS**, stem ends trimmed

1½ tablespoons **FRESH LEMON JUICE**

⅓ cup **SLIVERED ALMONDS**, toasted (see Cook's Note, page 64)

Freshly ground **PEPPER**

In a small skillet over medium heat, melt 2 tablespoons of the butter. Add the *panko* and toast, stirring constantly, for about 2 minutes until golden brown and crisp. Remove from the heat and stir in the lemon zest and a pinch of salt. Set aside.

Fill a large saucepan two-thirds full of water and bring to a boil over high heat. Add 1 tablespoon of salt. Add the beans and cook for about 2 minutes until bright green and still very crisp. Meanwhile, fill a large bowl two-thirds full of ice water. Using tongs or a slotted spoon, immediately transfer the beans to the ice water. Let cool in the water for 2 minutes and then drain thoroughly, blot dry with paper towels, and set aside.

In a 12-inch skillet over medium-high heat, melt the remaining 3 tablespoons butter and swirl to coat the pan. Add the green beans and sauté, stirring constantly, for about 3 minutes until the beans are heated through and crisp-tender. Add the lemon juice and almonds and sauté for 1 minute longer. Season to taste with salt and pepper. Transfer to a warmed serving bowl. Sprinkle with the *panko* topping and serve immediately.

DO AHEAD

This sauté is best when made right before serving. However, the green beans can be blanched up to 1 day in advance. Spread the cooled beans on dry paper towels or a clean cotton towel, roll up jelly-roll style, and place in a sealed plastic bag. Remove from the refrigerator 2 hours before sautéing. The *panko* topping and toasted almonds can be prepared up to 1 day in advance. Cover and store in separate airtight containers at room temperature.

Creamed Pearl Onions
with Bacon

SERVES 8 TO 10

For many families, creamed onions are almost as traditional as turkey on the Thanksgiving table. There are lots of variations; my favorite includes the addition of bacon and fresh thyme and parsley, not only for a savory taste, but also for the visual appeal of flecks of green herbs against the creamy white sauce and onions.

2 pounds **PEARL ONIONS** (do not peel; see Cook's Note)

2½ teaspoons **KOSHER OR SEA SALT,** plus more for seasoning

4 strips **BACON,** cut into ¼-inch dice

1 tablespoon **UNSALTED BUTTER**

¼ teaspoon **SWEET PAPRIKA**

1¼ cups **HALF-AND-HALF,** warmed

2 teaspoons **FRESH THYME LEAVES**

¼ cup minced **FRESH FLAT-LEAF PARSLEY**

Pinch of freshly grated **NUTMEG**

Freshly ground **PEPPER**

Fill a large saucepan two-thirds full with water and bring to a boil over medium-high heat. Add the onions and 2 teaspoons of the salt. Boil the onions for 10 to 12 minutes until tender. Drain and rinse under cold running water, then drain again. Cut off the root ends and squeeze at the stem ends to slip the onions from their skins. Set aside.

In a 10-inch sauté pan, cook the bacon over medium heat for about 5 minutes until crisp. Using a slotted spoon, transfer the bacon to a plate lined with paper towels to drain. Pour off the bacon fat, reserving 1½ teaspoons. Wipe out the pan.

Using the same pan, melt the butter over medium heat. Add the reserved bacon fat and the paprika and whisk just until blended. Add the half-and-half and cook, whisking constantly, for about 2 minutes until the sauce is smooth and slightly thickened. Add the thyme, parsley, and remaining ½ teaspoon salt; stir to blend. Add the onions and bacon and cook for about 3 minutes until heated through. Add the nutmeg, and then season to taste with pepper. Serve immediately, or cover and set aside for up to 1 hour. Reheat gently just before serving.

COOK'S NOTE I prefer to use fresh pearl onions, and most markets have them during the holiday season. However, frozen pearl onions are a reasonable substitute. They are already peeled and blanched. Boil the onions just until heated through. Drain them thoroughly before adding to the sauce.

DO AHEAD The onions can be cooked up to 1 day in advance. Cover and refrigerate. Bring to room temperature before making the sauce.

Cracked Pepper and Butter Peas with Parmesan

SERVES 8 TO 10

Fresh peas, especially organically grown ones, picked in season when sweet and tender and then flash frozen, are a classic accompaniment to roast turkey and gravy. The peas are brought into a contemporary light when seasoned with fresh cracked pepper and showered with freshly-grated Parmigiano-Reggiano cheese.

1 cup **HOMEMADE CHICKEN STOCK** (see page 11) **OR CANNED LOW-SODIUM CHICKEN BROTH**

3 cups **FROZEN PEAS**

2 tablespoons **UNSALTED BUTTER**, melted

KOSHER OR SEA SALT

Coarsely ground **BLACK PEPPERCORNS**

⅓ cup (1½ ounces) freshly grated **PARMESAN CHEESE**, preferably Parmigiano-Reggiano

In a medium saucepan, bring the chicken stock and 2 cups of water to a boil over high heat. Add the peas and cook for 1 to 2 minutes just until the peas turn bright green. Remove from the heat, drain all the liquid, and transfer to a warm serving bowl. Toss the peas with the butter, season with salt and a generous amount of freshly cracked pepper. Scatter the Parmesan over top and serve immediately.

DO AHEAD

The peas are best when cooked right before serving. Have the stock and water simmering and the other ingredients measured and ready.

Sautéed Brussels Sprouts with Smoked Ham and Toasted Pecans

SERVES 8 TO 10

Brussels sprouts are one of the most maligned winter vegetables, probably because they are often cooked so poorly. They are usually served whole, overcooked, and underflavored—but this need not be the case. Simply trimming and halving the Brussels sprouts, or better yet shredding them, brings out the flavor inside these tightly, delicately layered orbs. Diced smoked ham and toasted pecans add flavor and crunch.

2 pounds **BRUSSELS SPROUTS**

2 tablespoons **UNSALTED BUTTER**

3 tablespoons **EXTRA-VIRGIN OLIVE OIL**

1 large clove **GARLIC**, finely minced

One ⅛-inch-thick slice **SMOKED HAM**, coarsely chopped

⅔ cup **HOMEMADE CHICKEN STOCK** (see page 11) **OR CANNED LOW-SODIUM CHICKEN BROTH**

Pinch of **SUGAR**

KOSHER OR SEA SALT

Freshly ground **PEPPER**

½ cup coarsely chopped toasted **PECANS** (see Cook's Note, page 64)

Trim the stem end of the Brussels sprouts and remove any yellow or spotted outer leaves. Cut the Brussels sprouts into very thin slices about ¹⁄₁₆ inch thick, and use your fingertips to separate the slices into shreds. Alternatively, shred the Brussels sprouts using a food processor with the coarse shredding disk attached. Place in a bowl and set aside until ready to sauté.

In a 14-inch sauté pan, melt the butter with the olive oil over medium heat and swirl to coat the pan. Add the garlic and sauté for about 1 minute until soft but not browned. Add the Brussels sprouts and sauté for about 3 minutes until bright green and barely crisp-tender. Raise the heat to high and add the ham and stock. Stir to blend, cover the pan, and steam for about 2 minutes longer until the Brussels sprouts are crisp-tender. Season with a little sugar, salt, and pepper. Transfer to a warmed serving bowl and top with the toasted pecans. Serve immediately.

DO AHEAD

This sauté is best when made right before serving. However, the ingredients can be prepared and chopped up to 8 hours in advance. Cover the prepared Brussels sprouts, garlic, and pecans and set aside at room temperature. Chop the ham and place it in a covered container in the refrigerator.

Framboise Cranberry Sauce

MAKES ABOUT 2¼ CUPS
This recipe was given to me by Lisa Morrison, one of the talented students in the six-week food-writing course that I teach each year in Portland, Oregon, where I live. I was developing recipes for a Christmas cookbook while teaching the course and Lisa offered to give me her favorite recipe for cranberry relish, which calls for a 12-ounce bottle of framboise Lambic, a raspberry-flavored Belgian beer. Not surprisingly, I was skeptical, but Lisa writes extensively about beer for many publications and is known locally as "the beer goddess," so it was worth a try. The recipe worked beautifully, the relish tastes terrific, and it is a fun twist on the traditional cranberry relish served with the holiday bird.

1 bottle (12 ounces) **LINDEMANS FRAMBOISE LAMBIC BEER**

1 package (12 ounces) **FRESH OR THAWED FROZEN CRANBERRIES**, picked over and stems removed

¼ cup finely diced **CRYSTALLIZED GINGER** (see Cook's Note)

¼ cup **SUGAR**

In a deep, 4-quart saucepan over medium-high heat, bring the beer to a boil. Add the cranberries, ginger, and sugar. Reduce the heat to maintain a simmer and stir to dissolve the sugar. Cook, stirring occasionally, for about 10 minutes until the cranberries begin to pop open. Remove from the heat and let cool to room temperature. Transfer the cooled relish to a bowl, cover, and refrigerate until ready to serve.

COOK'S NOTE Crystallized ginger slices are typically packaged in 4-ounce boxes and are available in the Asian- foods section of well-stocked supermarkets. I've also seen diced crystallized ginger sold in vacuum-sealed cans in the baking section of grocery stores.

DO AHEAD The relish can be made up to 10 days in advance. Store in a tightly covered container in the refrigerator.

Cape Cod Cranberry Compote

MAKES ABOUT 2½ CUPS

Early New England cookbooks suggested that a darning needle be used to pierce the stem end of each cranberry and run the needle through the berry in order to keep the fruit from bursting when cooked. Darning needles seem to have gone out of style along with the laborious process of piercing each cranberry. Gentle simmering will keep most of the berries whole and retain the desired texture of a compote rather than a sauce. In the Yankee spirit, add a touch of applejack to spike the flavor once the compote has cooled down. I purchased Laird's applejack at my local liquor store. Laird's, the country's oldest distiller, makes applejack from tree-ripened apples grown in the Shenandoah Valley orchards. The pressed juice is fermented, distilled, and then aged for 4 to 8 years.

1½ cups **WATER**

1½ cups **SUGAR**

1 package (12 ounces) **FRESH CRANBERRIES**, picked over and stems removed

Juice of ½ **LEMON**

1 tablespoon freshly grated **ORANGE ZEST**

3 tablespoons **APPLEJACK BRANDY**, or more to taste

In a deep, 4-quart saucepan, combine the water and sugar and bring to a boil over medium-high heat. Reduce the heat to maintain a simmer and cook for about 10 minutes until the mixture is syrupy. Add the cranberries, lemon juice, and orange zest. Adjust the heat so the mixture barely simmers and cook, stirring occasionally, for about 10 minutes until the cranberries just begin to pop open and the syrup thickens. Remove from the heat and let cool to room temperature. Add the applejack. Transfer the compote to a bowl, cover, and refrigerate. Remove from the refrigerator 1 hour before serving.

DO AHEAD   The compote can be made up to 10 days in advance. Store in a tightly covered container in the refrigerator. Remove from the refrigerator 1 hour before serving.

Fresh Cranberry Salsa

MAKES ABOUT 3 CUPS

Sukey Garcetti, a friend from Los Angeles, shared recipes from her family's Mexican Thanksgiving menu. Her husband, Gil, although having an Italian surname, is mostly of Mexican descent and comes from a family of talented cooks. Reinterpreting salsa, using cranberries instead of tomatoes, is a terrific, nontraditional spin on cranberry sauce. While Gil's mother chopped everything by hand, I took the liberty of grinding the cranberries in the processor, but I do prefer the look of the celery, onion, and jalapeño diced by hand. Include the seeds and ribs from the jalapeño if you like your salsa spicier, or use a serrano chile instead of a jalapeño.

1 package (12 ounces) **FRESH CRANBERRIES**, picked over and stems removed

2 large ribs **CELERY**, finely diced

1 small **WHITE ONION**, finely diced

1 **JALAPEÑO CHILE**, seeded, deribbed, and minced (see Cook's Note, page 40)

¼ cup chopped **FRESH CILANTRO**

½ teaspoon **KOSHER OR SEA SALT**

¾ cup **SUGAR**

3 tablespoons **FRESH LIME JUICE**

In a food processor fitted with the metal blade, process the cranberries until coarsely and evenly chopped. Transfer to a medium bowl. Add the celery, onion, chile, cilantro, salt, sugar, and lime juice. Stir well to combine. Transfer to a serving bowl, cover, and refrigerate until ready to serve.

DO AHEAD

The salsa is best if made at least 3 hours or up to 1 day in advance to allow the flavors to meld. Store in a tightly covered container in the refrigerator.

Desserts

Dessert, that much-anticipated finale to our Thanksgiving meal, was probably not served at the first Thanksgiving. Recipes for pumpkin pie didn't appear until later in the 17th century, and ovens necessary for pie baking weren't yet available to colonial cooks. These days, no matter how long or how filling the meal might be, no holiday get-together is complete without scrumptious desserts. Expand your end-of-meal repertoire with offerings that evoke a regional theme, including Indiana Persimmon Pudding, Key Lime Custard Tart, and Bourbon Pecan Pie with Buttermilk Whipped Cream.

Apple-Raisin Pie
with a Pastry Leaf Crust

**MAKES ONE 10-INCH PIE;
SERVES 8 TO 10**

My family is always split over what pie should be served for Thanksgiving; my daughter adores pumpkin pie; my son always wants a fruit pie; and my husband likes both, but especially wants enough so there are leftovers for our leisurely breakfast the morning after Thanksgiving. I learned, over the years, to make two pies, sometimes three, to satisfy everyone. It's a joy because I love rolling dough, getting my apron dusty with flour, and perfuming the house with the sweet smell of pies baking first thing Thanksgiving morning. I've also learned the convenience of making and freezing the dough two weeks ahead. I make the apple filling a day in advance and also put the dough in the refrigerator to thaw. This makes pie assembly a snap on Thanksgiving morning.

Pie Crust

2½ cups **ALL-PURPOSE FLOUR**,
  plus extra for dusting

1 teaspoon **KOSHER OR SEA SALT**

2 teaspoons **GRANULATED SUGAR**

½ cup (1 stick) ice-cold **UNSALTED
  BUTTER**, cut into small pieces

½ cup ice-cold **SOLID VEGETABLE
  SHORTENING** or **LEAF LARD**
  (see Headnote, page 132)

⅓ cup **SOUR CREAM**

2 tablespoons **ICE WATER**

•• CONTINUED ••

To make the crust, combine the 2½ cups flour, the salt, and granulated sugar in a food processor fitted with the metal blade. Add the butter and shortening and pulse until the mixture resembles coarse meal. Add the sour cream and water and process for a few seconds, just until a ball of dough begins to form. Do not overprocess. (To make the dough by hand, place the dry ingredients in a large bowl, and use a pastry blender to cut the butter and shortening into the flour mixture. Add the sour cream and ice water, and mix just until it comes together and forms a mass.)

Transfer the dough to a floured work surface, gathering all the loose bits, and form into a disk about 1 inch thick. Cut the dough into 2 pieces, wrap each piece in plastic wrap, and refrigerate for at least 30 minutes, or up to overnight.

To make the filling, in a small bowl, combine the raisins and rum. Let stand to macerate while you prepare the apples. In a large bowl, combine the apples, butter, brown sugar, flour, cinnamon, and nutmeg. Mix thoroughly to dissolve the sugar and blend in the spices. Add the raisins and any liquid from the bowl and stir to combine. Set aside.

Position a rack in the center of the oven and place another rack under it. Preheat the oven to 400°F. Have a 10-inch pie pan ready.

•• CONTINUED ••

Filling

½ cup **RAISINS**

2 tablespoons **DARK RUM OR BOURBON WHISKEY**

7 **GOLDEN DELICIOUS APPLES** (about 3 pounds total weight), peeled, cored, and cut into ½-inch wedges

4 tablespoons (½ stick) **UNSALTED BUTTER**, melted

¾ cup firmly packed **GOLDEN BROWN SUGAR**

1 tablespoon **ALL-PURPOSE FLOUR**

1½ teaspoons **GROUND CINNAMON**

¼ teaspoon freshly grated **NUTMEG**

2 tablespoons **MILK**

1 tablespoon **TURBINADO SUGAR** (see Cook's Note) **OR GRANULATED SUGAR**

To assemble the pie, on a lightly floured work surface, roll out 1 piece of the dough into a circle about 12 inches in diameter. (Dust the work surface and dough with a little more flour as necessary to keep the dough from sticking.) Roll the dough around the rolling pin, lift it over the pie pan, and unroll the dough over the pan. Adjust to center the dough, then press it into place. Trim the excess dough, leaving a ½-inch overhang; then tuck it under itself to form a double thickness around the edge of the pan. Refrigerate the crust. Save any scraps of dough.

Roll out the remaining dough into a circle about ⅛ inch thick. Using a 2-inch maple-leaf or other leaf-shaped cutter, cut out leaf shapes from the dough. Roll the dough again, incorporating the scraps from the bottom crust, to cut more leaves. Arrange the leaves on a baking sheet and refrigerate until firm, about 10 minutes.

Spoon the filling into the pie shell, mounding it in the center. Using a small pastry brush dipped in the milk, moisten the edges of the bottom crust and the pastry leaves. Starting at the center of the pie, decoratively arrange the leaves, slightly overlapping, over the apples to form a top crust. (There will be some spaces between the leaves with apple showing through, which will allow steam to escape.) Lightly press together the leaves that overlap the bottom crust edges. Sprinkle the leaves and edges with the turbinado sugar.

Place the pie in the center of the oven, and place a rimmed baking sheet on the rack below. Bake for about 50 minutes until the crust is golden brown. Transfer to a wire rack and let cool. Serve the pie warm or at room temperature.

COOK'S NOTE   Turbinado sugar is usually available in the baking supplies aisle of a large super-market. It is light brown and has large crystals. Use it to sprinkle on muffins, scones, and pies just before baking.

DO AHEAD   The pie dough can made, wrapped tightly, and frozen up to 3 weeks in advance. Thaw overnight in the refrigerator before rolling it out. The bottom crust and pastry leaves can be rolled out up to 1 day in advance. Cover tightly with plastic wrap and refrigerate. The filling can be made up to 1 day in advance. Place in a covered container and refrigerate. The pie is best when baked the day you are planning to serve it.

Spiced Pumpkin Layer Cake with Cream Cheese Frosting

SERVES 12

When it comes to dessert, I am a chocoholic first and fruit-pie lover second; but after several test batches to perfect this cake, I am completely won over, and so is everyone who has tasted it. This is simply a spectacular cake—moist and light with spiced pumpkin flavor and sweet bites of coconut and pineapple. In addition, it is a snap to make. It requires two 9-inch cake pans to make the layers, but the cake itself can be mixed together with a rubber spatula and bowl. If all the cake ingredients are premeasured and the cake pans prepared, this can be a fun kitchen project to do with children, especially since it can be made ahead and frozen.

Cake

BUTTER for coating cake pans, at room temperature

2 cups **ALL-PURPOSE FLOUR**, plus extra for dusting the pan

2 cups **GRANULATED SUGAR**

2 teaspoons **BAKING SODA**

2 teaspoons **GROUND CINNAMON**

1 teaspoon **KOSHER OR SEA SALT**

½ teaspoon freshly grated **NUTMEG**

¼ teaspoon **GROUND CLOVES**

3 large **EGGS**, beaten

1 cup **CANOLA OR VEGETABLE OIL**

2 teaspoons **PURE VANILLA EXTRACT**

•• CONTINUED ••

Position a rack in the center of the oven and preheat to 350°F. Butter two 9-inch diameter cake pans with 1½-inch sides. Line the bottom of each pan with a circle of parchment paper. Butter the parchment paper. Sprinkle the pans with flour, tap the pans to evenly distribute the flour, and then shake off the excess flour. Set aside.

To make the cake, in a large bowl, sift together the 2 cups flour, the granulated sugar, baking soda, cinnamon, salt, nutmeg, and cloves. In a medium bowl, combine the eggs, oil, and vanilla. In another medium bowl, combine the pumpkin purée, coconut, crushed pineapple, and currants.

Add the egg mixture to the flour mixture and stir with a wooden spoon until just combined. Add the pumpkin mixture and stir just until combined. Divide the batter between the prepared pans, spreading it evenly. Bake for 35 to 40 minutes until a toothpick inserted into the center of a cake comes out clean. Transfer to wire racks and let cool in the pans for 15 minutes. Run a table knife around the edge of the pans to loosen the cakes. Invert the cakes onto the racks and peel off the parchment paper. Let cool completely before frosting the cakes.

•• CONTINUED ••

1¼ cups **CANNED UNSWEETENED PUMPKIN PURÉE**

1 cup lightly packed **SWEETENED FLAKED COCONUT**

¾ cup canned **CRUSHED PINEAPPLE** (do not drain)

⅓ cup **DRIED CURRANTS**

Cream Cheese Frosting

2 packages (8 ounces each) **CREAM CHEESE** at room temperature

1 cup (2 sticks) **UNSALTED BUTTER** at room temperature

2 tablespoons **CANNED UNSWEETENED PUMPKIN PURÉE**

1½ cups **CONFECTIONERS' SUGAR**, sifted

1 teaspoon **PURE VANILLA EXTRACT**

To make the frosting, in the bowl of an electric mixer fitted with the paddle attachment, beat the cream cheese on medium speed for about 3 minutes until smooth. Add the butter and beat for about 2 minutes until combined. Add the pumpkin purée and beat until incorporated, about 1 minute. Add the confectioners' sugar and vanilla and beat for about 3 minutes until fluffy.

Place 1 cake layer on a cake plate or platter. Using an offset spatula, spread half of the frosting over the top of the first cake layer. Spread the frosting right to the edge of the top without frosting the sides of the cake. Carefully place the second cake on top, lining up the edges. Spread the remaining frosting over the top of the cake without frosting the sides. Swirl the frosting to decorate the top. Refrigerate the cake to set the frosting. Remove from the refrigerator 30 to 40 minutes before serving.

DO AHEAD   The cake can be made up to 2 days in advance. Refrigerate until cold, and then carefully cover with plastic wrap. The cake can also be wrapped tightly and frozen for up to 1 month. Let thaw in the refrigerator, for about 12 hours.

Cranberry Cheesecake with a Chocolate-Cinnamon Crust

SERVES 10 TO 12

Though you might think this would be too heavy to include as a Thanksgiving dessert, I think of it as decadent and scrumptious, especially with the chocolate cinnamon crust and the tart, festive cranberry topping. Often, there is a delay between the main Thanksgiving meal and when dessert is served, which offers plenty of time to loosen the belt and make room for a slice of heavenly cheesecake. A boon to the Thanksgiving cook is that this dessert can be made in advance and frozen.

Crust

6 tablespoons **UNSALTED BUTTER**, melted

2 cups finely ground **CHOCOLATE WAFER COOKIES** (about 7 ounces of cookies; see Cook's Note)

1½ tablespoons **SUGAR**

2 teaspoons **GROUND CINNAMON**

¼ teaspoon **KOSHER OR SEA SALT**

Filling

3 packages **CREAM CHEESE** (8 ounces each), at room temperature

1 cup **SUGAR**

4 large **EGGS**, at room temperature

1 tablespoon **PURE VANILLA EXTRACT**

1 cup **SOUR CREAM**

To make the crust, position a rack in the center of the oven and preheat to 350°F. Using a pastry brush, butter a 9- or 10-inch springform pan with 1 tablespoon of the butter. In a medium bowl, combine the chocolate wafer crumbs, sugar, cinnamon, and salt. Blend in the remaining 5 tablespoons melted butter. Press the crumbs into the bottom and about 1 inch up the side of the prepared pan. (I use a ½-cup flat-bottomed, stainless-steel measuring cup to help press the crumbs into the bottom and sides of the pan, which helps prevent the corners from being thicker than the sides.) Bake the crust for about 8 to 10 minutes until crisp. Transfer to a wire rack to cool while you prepare the filling. (Press the bottom crust with the measuring cup again to gently smooth it.)

To make the filling, in the work bowl of a food processor fitted with the metal blade, process the cream cheese until smooth. Mix in the sugar, then add the eggs, one at a time, and continue processing until the mixture is thoroughly combined and creamy, scraping down the sides of the bowl once or twice. Add the vanilla and sour cream. Process until all the ingredients are thoroughly combined and the mixture is completely smooth. (Alternatively, beat the ingredients in a large bowl using an electric mixer.)

Topping

½ cup **WATER**

¾ cup **SUGAR**

1 package (12 ounces) **FRESH CRANBERRIES**, picked over and stems removed

2 teaspoons **CORNSTARCH** dissolved in 1 tablespoon water

Gently pour the cheesecake filling into the prebaked crust. The filling will likely rise above the crust, which is not a problem. Bake the cheesecake for about 40 minutes until the sides are slightly puffed. The center of the filling will still be very soft and will jiggle when you shake the pan gently. Turn off the oven and leave the cheesecake, undisturbed, in the oven with the door ajar, for 40 minutes. Transfer to a wire rack and let cool in the pan. Cover and refrigerate for at least 6 hours, or preferably overnight.

To make the topping, in a 2½-quart saucepan over medium-high heat, bring the water to a boil. Add the sugar and stir until the sugar is dissolved. Reduce the heat to medium and add the cranberries. Cook, stirring frequently, for about 3 minutes just until the berries begin to pop. Stir in the cornstarch mixture and simmer for 1 minute longer. Remove from the heat and let cool to room temperature. Cover and refrigerate for at least 4 hours before serving to allow the sauce to set.

COOK'S NOTE   Use Nabisco brand Famous Chocolate Wafers for the crust. Break the cookies into chunks and grind them in a food processor fitted with the metal blade to achieve even crumbs.

DO AHEAD   The cheesecake can be wrapped tightly and refrigerated for up to 3 days or frozen for up to 1 month. Let thaw in the refrigerator, for about 12 hours. The topping can be made up to 2 days in advance. Cover and refrigerate. Remove the topping from the refrigerator 2 hours before serving.

Key Lime Custard Tart

SERVES 8

This Key lime tart, non-traditional but refreshingly perfect after a big holiday feast, is creamy and mildly tangy with a custard consistency. It is spooned into a prebaked shortbread crust that is buttery tender, yet sturdy enough to not get soggy from the cream filling. The small Key lime, once predominantly grown in the Florida Keys, is now cultivated in Texas, California, Mexico, and Central America. Use those if you find them in the market; otherwise the larger, traditional Persian limes work fine.

Shortbread Crust

¾ cup (1½ sticks) **UNSALTED BUTTER**, removed from the refrigerator 30 minutes before preparing crust, cut into small cubes

⅓ cup sifted **CONFECTIONERS' SUGAR**

1 teaspoon freshly grated **LIME ZEST**

¼ teaspoon **KOSHER OR SEA SALT**

1½ cups **ALL-PURPOSE FLOUR**, plus extra for dusting

Custard Filling

6 large **EGGS**

¾ cup **HEAVY (WHIPPING) CREAM**

1 cup **GRANULATED SUGAR**

2 teaspoons freshly grated **LIME ZEST**

⅔ cup **FRESH LIME JUICE**

1 to 2 **LIMES**, cut into paper-thin rounds

CONFECTIONERS' SUGAR for dusting

To make the crust, in the bowl of an electric mixer fitted with the paddle attachment, beat the butter, confectioners' sugar, and lime zest on medium speed until smooth and creamy, for about 2 minutes. Add the salt and 1½ cups flour and mix on low speed just until the flour disappears, scraping down the sides of the bowl once with a rubber spatula. Do not overmix. The dough should look dry. Form the dough into a flat disk about ¾ inch thick and wrap in plastic wrap. Refrigerate the dough for 30 minutes.

Transfer the dough to a lightly floured work surface. Dust the top of the dough with flour. Using a lightly floured rolling pin, roll the dough out to a 12-inch round about ⅛ inch thick. Fit the dough into a standard 10-inch fluted tart pan with a removable bottom. Trim away any excess dough and use a fork to prick the crust all over. Chill the dough for 30 minutes.

Position a rack in the center of the oven and preheat to 350°F. Line the shell with aluminum foil or parchment paper and fill with pie weights. Bake for about 20 minutes until the crust is pale golden and set. Carefully remove the foil and pie weights and bake for 5 minutes longer. Transfer to a wire rack and let cool completely before filling. Reduce the oven temperature to 300°F.

•• CONTINUED ••

To make the filling, in a large bowl, whisk the eggs until well beaten. Add the cream, granulated sugar, lime zest, and lime juice. Whisk until well combined. Carefully pour all but 1 cup of the filling into the tart shell. Set the tart on a rimmed baking sheet and place it on the rack in the oven. Use a small ladle to add the remaining filling to the tart shell. (Depending upon the exact size of the pan, you might end up with 2 to 4 tablespoons of filling left over.)

Bake the tart for 30 minutes. Turn the oven off and, without opening the door, leave the tart undisturbed for 30 minutes longer. The tart should be puffed at the edges and set in the center. Transfer to the wire rack and let cool in the pan. Refrigerate until well chilled, for at least 2 hours and up to 24 hours before serving.

When ready to serve, arrange the lime slices around the edge of the tart and dust the top of the tart generously with confectioners' sugar. Remove the side of the pan, cut into wedges, and serve.

DO AHEAD   The tart dough can be made and frozen up to 2 weeks in advance. Let thaw in the refrigerator, for about 12 hours. The tart shell can be baked up to 1 day in advance. Cover with foil and set aside at room temperature. The tart can be made completely up to 1 day in advance. Let cool, cover, and refrigerate until ready to serve.

Molasses Gingerbread Cake with Cinnamon Whipped Cream

SERVES 10 TO 12

According to *The New England Yankee Cook Book*, written by Imogene Wolcott and published in 1939, more gingerbread is eaten in New England than in any other section of the country. It was probably one of the first breads baked in New England. A gingerbread recipe was brought over on the *Mayflower*. Many thanks to my friend and cookbook author David Lebovitz for sharing his recipe. I've never made a gingerbread cake as good as this one.

Cake

1 tablespoon **UNSALTED BUTTER** at room temperature

3¾ cups **ALL-PURPOSE FLOUR**, plus extra for dusting pan

1½ teaspoons **GROUND CINNAMON**

¾ teaspoon **GROUND CLOVES**

¾ teaspoon freshly ground **PEPPER**

1½ cups **SWEET UNSULPHURED MOLASSES** (not blackstrap)

1½ cups **GRANULATED SUGAR**

1½ cups **CANOLA OR PEANUT OIL**

1½ cups **WATER**

1 tablespoon **BAKING SODA**

⅔ cup (packed), peeled and minced **FRESH GINGER** (see Cook's Note)

3 large **EGGS**, beaten

•• CONTINUED ••

Position a rack in the lower third of the oven and preheat to 350°F. Generously butter and flour a nonstick, 12-cup Bundt pan, tapping the pan over the sink to remove excess flour. (Make certain every interior surface is thoroughly coated so the cake doesn't stick.)

To make the cake, in a large bowl, sift together the 3¾ cups flour, the cinnamon, cloves, and pepper. In another large bowl, whisk together the molasses, granulated sugar, and oil.

In a 2½-quart saucepan, bring the water to a boil. Remove from the heat and stir in the baking soda. Whisk this mixture into the molasses mixture, and then add the fresh ginger.

Adding a generous cupful at a time, stir the flour mixture into the molasses mixture, until the flour is absorbed. Whisk in the eggs. Pour the batter into the prepared pan.

Bake the cake for about 1 hour until a toothpick inserted into the center of the cake comes out clean. If the cake appears to be browning too quickly, lay a piece of foil over the top of the pan. Transfer the cake to a wire rack and let cool in the pan for 1 hour. Place the rack over the top of the pan and invert to unmold the cake. Let the cake continue to cool on the rack.

•• CONTINUED ••

Cinnamon Whipped Cream

1½ cups **HEAVY (WHIPPING) CREAM**

¼ cup **CONFECTIONERS' SUGAR**

½ teaspoon **GROUND CINNAMON**

CONFECTIONERS' SUGAR for dusting

To make the whipped cream, combine the cream, confectioners' sugar, and cinnamon in a medium bowl. Using a whisk or electric mixer whip the cream until soft peaks form. Cover and refrigerate until ready to serve.

To serve, using a small fine-mesh sieve, dust the confectioners' sugar over the cake. Cut the cake into slices. Place a slice of cake in the center of each plate, top with a dollop of the whipped cream, and serve immediately.

COOK'S NOTE   You'll need to buy about 5 to 6 ounces of fresh ginger in order to have ⅔ cup of minced ginger. The easiest way to prepare the ginger is to peel it, cut it into small chunks, and mince it in a mini food processor or in a regular-size food processor using the metal blade. It certainly can be minced by hand; it just takes longer to prepare.

DO AHEAD   The cake can be covered and stored at room temperature for up to 2 days, or wrap tightly and freeze for up to 1 month. Thaw overnight at room temperature. The whipped cream can be prepared up to 4 hours in advance. Cover and refrigerate until ready to serve.

Bourbon Pecan Pie with Buttermilk Whipped Cream

SERVES 8 TO 10   Whether you are using Texas or Georgia pecans, this is simply the best pecan pie I have ever tasted. Pecan pies are too often sickeningly sweet. The secret here is brown rice syrup, which is readily available in natural food stores. I happen to think the booze helps, too. Add a little more to the whipped cream if you like.

Pie Crust

1¼ cups **ALL-PURPOSE FLOUR**, plus extra for dusting

½ teaspoon **KOSHER OR SEA SALT**

2 teaspoons **GRANULATED SUGAR**

4 tablespoons (½ stick) ice-cold **UNSALTED BUTTER**, cut into small pieces

¼ cup ice-cold **SOLID VEGETABLE SHORTENING**, cut into small pieces

3 tablespoons **SOUR CREAM**

1 tablespoon **ICE WATER**

Filling

3 large **EGGS**, lightly beaten

1 cup **BROWN RICE SYRUP** (see Cook's Note)

3 tablespoons **PURE MAPLE SYRUP**

2 tablespoons **BOURBON WHISKEY**

3 tablespoons **UNSALTED BUTTER**, melted

¼ teaspoon **KOSHER OR SEA SALT**

2 cups **PECAN HALVES**

•• CONTINUED ••

To make the crust, combine the 1¼ cups flour, the salt, and graunlated sugar in a food processor fitted with the metal blade. Scatter the butter and shortening pieces over the flour mixture and pulse until the mixture resembles coarse meal. Add the sour cream and water and process for a few seconds, just until a ball of dough begins to form. Do not overprocess. (To make the dough by hand, place the dry ingredients in a large bowl and use a pastry blender or 2 knives to cut the butter and shortening into the flour mixture. Add the sour cream and ice water and mix just until it comes together and forms a mass.)

Transfer the dough to a floured work surface, gathering all the loose bits, and form into a disk about 1 inch thick. Wrap the dough in plastic wrap and refrigerate for at least 30 minutes, or up to overnight.

Have a 9- or 10-inch pie pan ready. On a lightly floured work surface, roll out the dough into a circle about 12 inches in diameter. Dust the work surface and dough with a little more flour, as necessary, to keep the dough from sticking. Roll the dough around the rolling pin, lift it over the pie pan, and unroll the dough over the pan. Adjust to center the dough, then press it into place. Trim the excess dough, leaving a ½-inch overhang; then tuck it under itself to form a double thickness around the edge of the pan. Crimp the edges with a fork, or use your fingers to flute the edges to form a decorative pie crust. Refrigerate the crust while you make the filling. Position a rack in the center of the oven and preheat to 400°F.

To make the filling, in a large bowl, combine the eggs, brown rice syrup, maple syrup, bourbon, butter, and salt. Whisk until smooth. Fold in the pecans and set aside.

•• CONTINUED ••

1 tablespoon **MILK**

Buttermilk Whipped Cream

1 cup **HEAVY (WHIPPING) CREAM**

⅓ cup **BUTTERMILK**

2 tablespoons **CONFECTIONERS' SUGAR**

To assemble the pie, pour the pecan filling into the chilled pie shell. Use a pastry brush to brush some of the milk along the edge of the pastry. Place the pie in the oven, and immediately reduce the temperature to 350°F. Bake the pie for about 40 to 45 minutes until the filling just begins to puff at the edges and the center no longer jiggles when gently shaken. Transfer to a wire rack and let cool completely.

To make the whipped cream, in a medium bowl, combine the cream, buttermilk, and confectioners' sugar. Using a whisk or an electric mixer, whip the cream until soft peaks form. Cover and refrigerate until ready to serve.

Slice the pie into wedges, top with the buttermilk whipped cream, and serve.

COOK'S NOTE   Brown rice syrup is a sweetener. Light brown in color, it is only moderately sweet compared to corn syrup. For those with wheat allergies, it has the advantage of being gluten free. Brown rice syrup is typically sold in glass jars and is found in the baking section of natural food stores.

DO AHEAD   The pie dough can be made, wrapped tightly, and frozen up to 3 weeks in advance. Thaw overnight in the refrigerator before rolling it out. The whipped cream can be prepared up to 4 hours in advance. Cover and refrigerate until ready to serve. The pie is best when baked the day you are planning to serve it.

Indiana Persimmon Pudding

SERVES 12 TO 16

Although native to the southeastern United States, persimmons grow wild over much of southern Indiana and Illinois. In autumn, persimmon trees hang heavy with these glowing orange fruits. Their luscious fruit is ready to eat when it is soft and squashy-dead ripe. The native, or American, persimmon (*Diospyros virginiana*) is considered a real delicacy by southern Indiana residents and is eaten both fresh and cooked in dishes such as this classic pudding. This wasn't a tradition in my family growing up, but once I made the pudding for Thanksgiving, my family became totally hooked. In fact, I caught my husband and children rewarming the pudding for breakfast the day after Thanksgiving. While the pudding is plenty rich as is, it's traditional to serve a dollop of whipped cream on the side, even at breakfast!

In the South and Midwest, the American persimmon is readily found in the market during the fall. Those who live on the East and West Coasts are more likely to find two varieties of the Japanese persimmon (*Diospyros kaki*); one type, the Hachiya, is heart shaped with a pointed base, and the other, the Fuyu, is smaller and more spherical. Use the Hachiya variety for this recipe. The fruit needs to be exceedingly ripe—so soft to the touch that it would land with a splat if dropped on the ground.

1 tablespoon **BUTTER** at room temperature for buttering pan

2 cups **PERSIMMON PULP** (about 8)

2 cups **GRANULATED SUGAR**

2 large **EGGS**, lightly beaten

1 teaspoon **PURE VANILLA EXTRACT**

•• CONTINUED ••

Preheat the oven to 350°F. Butter a 9-by-13-inch baking pan. Cut the persimmons in half crosswise and use a spoon to scoop out the flesh, discarding the stem and skins. Use the back of a spoon to press the flesh into a soft pulp. Measure out 2 cups (refrigerate or freeze the rest and reserve for another use). Combine the 2 cups pulp, the granulated sugar, eggs, and vanilla in a medium bowl.

•• CONTINUED ••

1¾ cups **ALL-PURPOSE FLOUR**

1 teaspoon **BAKING SODA**

1 teaspoon **BAKING POWDER**

1 teaspoon **KOSHER OR SEA SALT**

1 teaspoon **GROUND CINNAMON**

1½ cups **BUTTERMILK**

½ cup **HEAVY (WHIPPING) CREAM**

2 tablespoons **UNSALTED BUTTER,** melted

CONFECTIONERS' SUGAR for dusting

In a large bowl, sift together the flour, baking soda, baking powder, salt, and cinnamon. Add the persimmon mixture, one-third at a time, beating well after each addition. Stir in the buttermilk, cream, and melted butter. Pour into the prepared pan and bake for about 45 minutes until nicely browned and slightly puffed at the edges. Serve warm or rewarm just before serving, dusted with the confectioners' sugar.

DO AHEAD   The persimmon pudding can be made up to 8 hours in advance. Cover loosely and set aside at room temperature. Rewarm just before serving.

Old-Fashioned Pumpkin Pie with Pecan Pastry Crust

MAKES TWO 9-INCH PIES; SERVES 16 TO 20

Pumpkin as an ingredient or pumpkin pudding has been around since the Pilgrims' second Thanksgiving in 1623, and there has been stiff competition out there ever since for the best pumpkin pie recipe. I have baked and sampled many, and this version is my favorite because of the delightful interplay between the smooth custard filling and the nutty flavor and crunch of the crust. You can't go wrong if you serve this pumpkin pie with rum or maple-flavored whipped cream or simply vanilla ice cream.

Pie Crust

2¼ cups **ALL-PURPOSE FLOUR**, plus extra for dusting

½ cup **PECANS**, (see Cook's Note, page 64) toasted, then finely ground

1 teaspoon **KOSHER OR SEA SALT**

1 tablespoon **GRANULATED SUGAR**

½ cup (1 stick) ice-cold **UNSALTED BUTTER**, cut into small pieces

½ cup ice-cold **SOLID VEGETABLE SHORTENING**, cut into small pieces

⅓ cup **SOUR CREAM**

2 tablespoons **ICE WATER**

Filling

3½ cups or 2 cans (15 ounces each) **UNSWEETENED PUMPKIN PURÉE**

7 large **EGGS**, lightly beaten

⅔ cup **UNSULPHURED MOLASSES**

⅓ cup **GRANUALTED SUGAR**

•• CONTINUED ••

To make the crust, combine the 2¼ cups flour, the pecans, salt, and granulated sugar in a food processor fitted with the metal blade. Scatter the butter and short-ening pieces over the flour mixture and pulse until the mixture resembles coarse meal. Add the sour cream and water and process for a few seconds, just until a ball of dough begins to form. Do not overprocess. (To make the dough by hand, place the dry ingredients in a large bowl, and use a pastry blender or 2 knives to cut the butter and shortening into the flour mixture. Add the sour cream and ice water, and mix just until the dough comes together and forms a mass.)

Transfer the dough to a floured work surface, gathering all the loose bits, and form into a disk about 1 inch thick. Cut the dough into 2 pieces, wrap each piece in plastic wrap, and refrigerate for at least 30 minutes, or up to overnight.

Have two 9-inch pie pans ready. On a lightly floured work surface, roll out 1 piece of the dough into a circle about 12 inches in diameter. Dust the work surface and dough with a little more flour, as necessary, to keep the dough from sticking. Roll the dough around the rolling pin, lift it over the pie pan, and unroll the dough over the pan. Adjust to center the dough, then press it into place. Trim the excess dough by running a knife around the edge of the pan. Repeat with the second piece of dough. Refrigerate the pie crusts while you make the decorative edge pieces.

Use a 1¼-inch decorative cookie cutter (such as a leaf, daisy, or star shape) to make cutouts from the dough trimmings. Reroll the scraps to make more cut-outs. You should have about 30 to 35 dough shapes per pie. Place in a single layer on a nonstick baking sheet and refrigerate.

•• CONTINUED ••

1 tablespoon **GROUND GINGER**

1 tablespoon **GROUND CINNAMON**

1 teaspoon freshly grated **NUTMEG**

½ teaspoon **GROUND ALLSPICE**

½ teaspoon **KOSHER OR SEA SALT**

½ teaspoon freshly ground **PEPPER**

2 cups **SOUR CREAM**

1 cup **HEAVY (WHIPPING) CREAM**

2 tablespoons **MILK**

SUGAR for sprinkling

Topping

1 cup **HEAVY (WHIPPING) CREAM**

2 tablespoons **CONFECTIONERS' SUGAR**

2 tablespoons **DARK RUM** or
   1 tablespoon **PURE MAPLE SYRUP**

To make the filling, in a large bowl, combine the pumpkin, eggs, molasses, granulated sugar, ginger, cinnamon, nutmeg, allspice, salt, and pepper. Whisk until smooth. Blend in the sour cream and heavy cream. Whisk until smooth and no white streaks are visible. Set aside.

Position a rack in the center of the oven and preheat to 350°F.

To assemble the pies, divide the pumpkin filling between the chilled pie shells. Use a pastry brush to brush milk on the edges of the pastry. Overlap the decorative cutouts around the edge of the pastry, pressing gently. There should be enough to circle each pan. Brush with milk and sprinkle with sugar. Bake the pies for about 40 minutes until the filling just begins to puff at the edges and the center no longer jiggles when gently shaken. Turn off the oven and leave the pies, undisturbed, in the oven with the door ajar, for 20 minutes. Transfer the pies to wire racks and let cool completely.

Meanwhile, make the topping: In a medium bowl, combine the cream, confectioners' sugar, and rum. Using a whisk or electric mixer, whip the cream until soft peaks form. Cover and refrigerate until ready to serve.

Slice the pies into wedges, top with whipped cream, and serve.

COOK'S NOTE   If you prefer to crimp the edges of the pumpkin pies rather than make decorative cutouts, instead of trimming the pastry to the edge of the pan, leave about 1 inch of overhang dough. Turn it under and crimp the edges to make a decorative border.

DO AHEAD   The pie dough can be made, wrapped tightly, and frozen up to 3 weeks in advance. Thaw overnight in the refrigerator before rolling it out. The filling can be made up to 1 day in advance. Place in a covered container and refrigerate. The whipped cream can be prepared up to 4 hours in advance. Cover and refrigerate until ready to serve. The pie is best when baked the day you are planning to serve it.

Cranberry-Cherry Crisp

SERVES 6 TO 8

If making pie seems daunting, let me suggest this easy-to-put-together crisp. A mound of hot fruit bubbling and oozing under a nutty topping is my idea of a warm winter dessert, especially after a big Thanksgiving meal. The tart cranberries play off the sweetness of the cherries, making a splendid, jewel-like pairing. Serve the crisp with a scoop of vanilla ice cream.

Topping

⅓ cup coarsely chopped **WALNUTS**, toasted (see Cook's Note, page 64)

½ cup **OLD-FASHIONED OATS**

½ cup **ALL-PURPOSE FLOUR**

⅓ cup firmly packed **GOLDEN BROWN SUGAR**

¾ teaspoon **GROUND CINNAMON**

½ teaspoon freshly grated **NUTMEG**

6 tablespoons (¾ stick) ice-cold **UNSALTED BUTTER**, cut into small pieces

Filling

1 package (12 ounces) **FRESH OR THAWED FROZEN CRANBERRIES**, picked over and stems removed

3 cups thawed **FROZEN PITTED DARK SWEET CHERRIES**

1 tablespoon **FRESH LEMON JUICE**

⅔ cup **GRANULATED SUGAR**

1 tablespoon **CORNSTARCH**

1 tablespoon **ALL-PURPOSE FLOUR**

Position a rack in the center of the oven and preheat to 375°F.

To make the topping, in a medium bowl, combine the nuts, oats, flour, brown sugar, cinnamon, and nutmeg. Scatter the butter pieces over the top. Using your fingers, blend the butter into the flour mixture until the mixture is crumbly. Set aside.

To make the filling, in a large bowl, combine the cranberries, cherries, and lemon juice. In a small bowl, combine the granulated sugar, cornstarch, and flour. Add the cornstarch mixture to the fruit, stirring gently to dissolve the sugar. Spoon the fruit into a 1½-quart baking dish.

Sprinkle the topping evenly over the fruit. Bake for about 40 minutes until the top is nicely browned and the fruit is bubbly. Serve warm.

DO AHEAD

The topping can be made up to 3 weeks in advance. Place the mixture in a lock-top plastic bag and freeze. Remove from the freezer 20 minutes before topping the crisp. The crisp is best made the day you plan to serve it.

Honey-Roasted Bosc Pears with Sticky Toffee Pudding Ice Cream

SERVES 10

This is a satisfying and simple dessert to follow a heavy Thanksgiving meal, or to serve as a fruit accompaniment to the **Molasses Gingerbread Cake with Cinnamon Whipped Cream** on page 175. The pears can be made ahead, which is a blessing to the harried Thanksgiving cook. I suggest decadent Sticky Toffee Pudding ice cream to serve with the pears, but choose whatever flavor suits your tastes.

6 tablespoons (¾ stick) **UNSALTED BUTTER**, melted

5 firm-ripe **BOSC PEARS**, halved lengthwise (leave stems intact), and cored

3 tablespoons **BALSAMIC VINEGAR**

⅔ cup **HONEY**

Freshly ground **PEPPER** (optional)

1 pint **STICKY-TOFFEE PUDDING ICE CREAM** or other toffee-flavored ice cream

Position a rack in the center of the oven and preheat to 400°F.

Pour the butter into a baking pan or rimmed baking sheet just large enough to hold the pears in a single layer. Tilt the pan to coat the bottom completely with the butter. Arrange the pears, cut sides down, in the butter. Roast for 20 to 25 minutes until tender when pierced with a knife.

In a small bowl, combine the vinegar and honey. Spoon the mixture over the pears and bake until bubbly hot, for about 5 minutes longer. To serve, arrange 1 pear half, cut side up, on each of 10 dessert plates and spoon some of the juices from the pan over top. If desired, grind some freshly ground pepper over top. Place a small scoop of ice cream next to the pear and serve immediately.

DO AHEAD

The pears can be roasted up to 8 hours in advance. Set aside at room temperature. Reheat in a 300°F oven for 10 minutes just before serving.

7

Leftover Favorites

Forget *déjà vu* all over again. Whether you want more time to visit with children who are home for the holidays or just crave a moment's pause before the next seasonal rush, create fabulous, inventive meals with Thanksgiving leftovers. Transform your holiday bounty into Heartland Turkey-and-Vegetable Chowder, Turkey and Andouille Sausage Gumbo, Yankee Turkey Pot Pie, or Classic Turkey Tetrazzini, an early twentieth-century pasta dish originally made with chicken and named after Italian-born opera star and gourmand Luisa Tetrazzini.

After-Thanksgiving
Turkey Stock

MAKES 4 TO 5 QUARTS

When it is time to clean up and put leftovers away after Thanksgiving dinner, my husband assigns himself the task of "dealing with the turkey." He carefully carves whatever meat is still left on the carcass and arranges it in a container. While doing this, he sips wine and picks at the carcass, nibbling on those delectable morsels of meat that cling to the bone, which is precisely why he likes this chore. He also offers to chop the carcass into large chunks and store it in a separate container—this delights me! Come Friday morning, while I'm shuffling around in slippers and workout clothes, drinking my coffee, I open the refrigerator and pull out the chopped carcass, ready for the stockpot. While some may head for the mall, ready to tackle their Christmas list, honestly, I'm happier lounging with the newspaper, watching the stock simmer.

1 meaty **TURKEY CARCASS,** chopped into large pieces

2 medium **CARROTS** (do not peel), cut into 2-inch chunks

1 large **YELLOW ONION** (do not peel), cut in half

2 large ribs **CELERY**, with leaves, cut into 2-inch chunks

1 teaspoon **BLACK PEPPERCORNS**

1 **BAY LEAF**

6 sprigs **FRESH PARSLEY**

2 sprigs **FRESH THYME**

Put the chopped turkey carcass in an 8-quart stockpot and add cold water to cover, leaving 2 inches of space at the top of the pot. Bring to a boil over medium-high heat, then reduce the heat to maintain a steady simmer. Using a large spoon or soup skimmer, skim off the brown foam that rises to the top. After 5 minutes or so, the foam will become white, and no more skimming will be necessary.

Add the carrots, onion, celery, peppercorns, bay leaf, parsley, and thyme. Partially cover the pot and adjust the heat so the stock barely simmers. Simmer the stock for at least 2 but preferably 4 hours, adding water, if necessary, to keep the bones covered.

Using a large slotted spoon, transfer the bones, meat, and vegetables to a large, fine-mesh sieve set over a large bowl to catch all the juices. Discard the solids. Pour the stock through the sieve into the large bowl. Let cool. (To cool the stock quickly, set the bowl in a larger one filled with ice water, or fill a sink with about 2 inches of ice water.) Stir the stock, occasionally, to help cool it down. Cover and refrigerate overnight.

The next day, lift and scrape the congealed fat from the surface using a large spoon. Discard the fat. Store the stock, covered, in the refrigerator and reheat when ready to use.

DO AHEAD The stock can be covered and stored in the refrigerator for up to 3 days. To keep longer, transfer to a freezer container or several small containers, allowing 1 inch of headspace, and freeze for up to 6 months.

Turkey, Black Bean, and Cumin Chili

SERVES 8 For chili lovers, here is a terrific way to utilize that leftover turkey. I start with dried black beans because the texture and taste of the chili is so much richer; however, the busy cook can make this chili with canned beans instead. Drain and rinse three 15-ounce cans of black beans. Follow the cooking directions, but simmer the chili for only 30 minutes.

1 pound **DRIED BLACK BEANS**

3 tablespoons **OLIVE OIL**

4 large cloves **GARLIC**, minced

2 large **YELLOW ONIONS**, chopped

1 large **YELLOW BELL PEPPER**, seeded, deribbed, and chopped

1 to 2 **JALAPEÑO CHILES**, seeded, deribbed, and minced (see page 40)

¼ cup **CHILI CON CARNE SEASONING OR CHILI POWDER**

2 tablespoons **GOLDEN BROWN SUGAR**

2 teaspoons **GROUND CUMIN**

1 teaspoon **GROUND CORIANDER**

1 teaspoon **DRIED THYME**

1 teaspoon **DRIED OREGANO**

Pick over the beans, removing any stones or other debris. Rinse the beans and set them aside.

In a large Dutch oven or other heavy-bottomed pot with a lid, heat the oil over medium heat. Add the garlic, onions, bell pepper, and chile and sauté, partially covered, stirring frequently, for about 5 minutes until soft but not browned. Add the chili con carne seasoning, brown sugar, cumin, coriander, thyme, and oregano. Stir and cook for 3 minutes longer.

1 can (28 ounces) **DICED TOMATOES IN JUICE**

4 to 5 cups **After-Thanksgiving Turkey Stock** (page 190) **OR CANNED LOW-SODIUM CHICKEN BROTH**

1 teaspoon **KOSHER OR SEA SALT**

2 cups diced **ROAST TURKEY** (½-inch dice)

Freshly ground **PEPPER**

4 tablespoons chopped **FRESH CILANTRO**

SOUR CREAM for garnish

Add the beans, tomatoes with their juice, 4 cups of the stock, and the salt. Bring to a boil, then reduce the heat to a simmer. Cover and cook for about 1½ hours until the beans are tender. Add the turkey and pepper. Add up to 1 cup of additional stock or broth to thin the chili to the desired consistency, if necessary. Taste and adjust the seasoning, adding additional salt, if needed.

Ladle into warmed bowls. Garnish each serving with ½ tablespoon of the cilantro and a dollop of sour cream and serve immediately.

DO AHEAD   Because chili freezes so well, I developed this recipe to make a big quantity, perfect for busy weeknight meals. Freeze in a covered container for up to 1 month.

Heartland Turkey-and-Vegetable Chowder

SERVES 8

This is a hearty, chock-full-of-vegetables chowder using leftover turkey. I make variations on this recipe throughout the winter when I have leftover chicken. See what's fresh in the produce aisle and feel free to vary the vegetables. You could use kale instead of Swiss chard, or even substitute spinach, adding it at the last minute. Add green beans in place of the zucchini, if desired. Serve this soup with a loaf of crusty French bread for a perfect one-course meal.

4 strips **BACON**, chopped

1 large **YELLOW ONION**, cut into ½-inch dice

2 large ribs **CELERY**, trimmed and cut into ½-inch dice

2 **CARROTS**, peeled and cut into ½-inch dice

2 large **RED POTATOES** (about 1 pound total weight), peeled and cut into ½-inch dice

1 small **BUTTERNUT SQUASH** (about 1 pound), peeled, halved lengthwise, seeded, and cut into ½-inch dice

8 cups **After-Thanksgiving Turkey Stock** (page 190) **OR CANNED LOW-SODIUM CHICKEN BROTH**

1 medium **ZUCCHINI**, cut into ½-inch dice

2 cups chopped deribbed **SWISS CHARD LEAVES**

2 cups diced **ROAST TURKEY** (½-inch dice)

1 tablespoon minced **FRESH SAGE**

1 tablespoon minced **FRESH THYME**

KOSHER OR SEA SALT

Freshly ground **PEPPER**

In a heavy 6- to 8-quart Dutch oven with a lid, cook the bacon over medium heat, stirring frequently, until crisp and browned. Remove with a slotted spoon to a plate lined with paper towels to drain. Pour off all but 3 tablespoons of the fat from the pan and return it to medium heat. Add the onion, celery, and carrots. Sauté, partially covered, stirring occasionally, for about 5 minutes until the vegetables are soft but not browned.

Add the potatoes, squash, and stock. Bring to a boil over medium-high heat, then reduce the heat to maintain a simmer. Partially cover the pot and cook for about 15 minutes until the potatoes and squash are tender. Add the zucchini, Swiss chard, turkey, sage, and thyme. Cook for 5 minutes longer. Add the bacon and season to taste with salt and pepper. Ladle the soup into warmed bowls and serve immediately. The soup can be made up to 2 days in advance. Cover and refrigerate.

New Mexico Turkey-Tortilla Soup

SERVES 6 This soup is simply amazing. With a completely different flavor profile than the Thanksgiving meal, it makes a fabulous Thanksgiving leftover. The thick broth is smoky-flavored and deeply rich from the addition of the ancho chile. It's not spicy hot, just bright tasting. Serve the soup in shallow bowls and pile high the crisp corn tortilla strips for a crunchy garnish.

CANOLA OIL for frying

Six 6-inch **CORN TORTILLAS**, halved and cut crosswise into ¼-inch strips

1 **DRIED ANCHO CHILE**, stemmed and seeded

1 **WHITE ONION**, chopped

3 cloves **GARLIC**, chopped

1 can (28 ounces) **PEELED, WHOLE PLUM TOMATOES**, drained

4 cups **After-Thanksgiving Turkey Stock** (page 190) **OR CANNED LOW-SODIUM CHICKEN BROTH**

2 cups shredded **ROAST TURKEY**

KOSHER OR SEA SALT

1 large **AVOCADO**, halved, pitted, flesh scooped out, and cut into ½-inch dice

6 ounces (1½ cups) **MEXICAN** *QUESO FRESCO* **CHEESE**, crumbled, or shredded **MONTEREY JACK**

⅓ cup lightly packed **CILANTRO LEAVES**

LIME WEDGES for serving

Pour the oil into an 8-inch heavy sauté pan to a depth of ½ inch. Place over medium-high heat and heat until the oil is shimmering (350°F on a deep-frying thermometer). In small batches, fry the tortilla strips, stirring them around, for about 1 minute until pale golden. (The oil will stop bubbling once they are crisp.) Using a slotted spoon, transfer the tortilla strips to a plate lined with paper towels. Reserve the oil.

Meanwhile, soak the chile in a small bowl of hot water for about 10 minutes until softened. Drain. Tear the chile into pieces. Set aside.

In a 6-quart saucepan, heat 2 tablespoons of the tortilla frying oil over medium heat. Add the onion and garlic and sauté, stirring frequently, for about 5 minutes until soft but not browned. Remove from the heat. Transfer the onions and garlic to a blender. Add the chile and the tomatoes. Blend to a smooth purée. Pour the purée back into the saucepan and return to medium heat. Add the stock or broth and bring to a simmer. Cover the pan and simmer the soup for 30 minutes. Stir in the shredded turkey. Taste and season with salt.

To serve, divide the avocado and cheese among 6 warmed shallow bowls. Ladle the soup over top and garnish with the tortilla strips and cilantro. Serve with lime wedges to squeeze over the top.

DO AHEAD The soup, without the turkey added, can be made up to 2 days in advance. Reheat gently and add the turkey just before serving.

Cast Iron Skillet Turkey Hash with Soft-Cooked Eggs

SERVES 6

There is no better or more enjoyable way to use up leftover turkey than to make turkey hash. This hash is wonderful for a weekend brunch or for an easy weeknight supper, especially after the big Thanksgiving meal. I like to serve the hash with a tossed green salad or a simple steamed vegetable and a crusty loaf of bread. Pass Tabasco or other hot sauce at the table; the vinegary, smoky flavor of hot sauce complements the turkey, tarragon, and runny soft-cooked eggs perfectly.

4 tablespoons (½ stick) **UNSALTED BUTTER**

2 pounds **RED-SKINNED, YUKON GOLD, OR YELLOW FINN POTATOES**, peeled and cut into ½-inch dice

1 large **YELLOW ONION**, cut into ½-inch dice

2 ribs **CELERY**, halved lengthwise, then cut crosswise into ½-inch-thick slices

1 large **RED BELL PEPPER**, seeded, deribbed, and cut into ½-inch dice

1 teaspoon **KOSHER OR SEA SALT**

½ teaspoon freshly ground **PEPPER**

3 cups coarsely chopped **ROAST TURKEY**

3 tablespoons chopped **FRESH TARRAGON**, plus extra for garnish

⅓ cup chopped **FRESH FLAT-LEAF PARSLEY**

6 large **EGGS**

TABASCO or other hot sauce

In a 12-inch skillet or sauté pan, preferably cast iron, melt the butter over medium heat and swirl to coat the pan. Add the potatoes and onion and sauté for about 1 minute until just coated with butter. Cover and cook for 7 minutes to steam the potatoes, stirring once. Add the celery and bell pepper, stir briefly, then cover and cook for 3 minutes longer. Uncover the pan, raise the heat to medium-high, and add the salt and pepper. Cook, stirring frequently, for about 10 minutes until the potatoes are lightly browned.

Gently fold in the turkey, tarragon, and parsley and cook for about 2 minutes just until the turkey is heated through. Using a large spoon, make 6 shallow depressions in the hash, spacing them equally around the pan, with one in the center. Carefully crack an egg into each hollowed-out spot. Cover the pan and cook the eggs for about 5 minutes until the whites are set and the yolks are still runny. Serve immediately, garnishing the top of each egg with a sprinkling of tarragon. Pass the hot sauce at the table.

DO AHEAD The potatoes and vegetables can be cooked and the potatoes browned up to 2 hours in advance. Set aside at room temperature.

Turkey and Andouille Sausage Gumbo

SERVES 8

In Louisiana, a big batch of gumbo is often made after Thanksgiving as a way to use up leftover turkey. This is a traditional recipe with the inclusion of fresh okra, andouille sausage (a Cajun smoked sausage), hot sauce, and filé powder. You could substitute *tasso*, a spiced smoked pork meat, for the sausage, if desired. Filé powder, the powdered leaves of the sassafras tree, is used when cooking authentic Cajun cuisine. It contributes a unique flavor to the gumbo but most importantly acts as a thickener. I found filé powder at a local gourmet grocer; otherwise, order it online at *www.thespicehouse.com* or *www.penzeys.com*.

3 strips **BACON**, cut into ½-inch dice

1 large **YELLOW ONION**, cut into ½-inch dice

1 large **GREEN PEPPER**, cut into ½-inch dice

2 large cloves **GARLIC**, minced

2 large ribs **CELERY**, trimmed and cut into ½-inch dice

8 cups **After-Thanksgiving Turkey Stock** (page 190) **OR CANNED LOW-SODIUM CHICKEN BROTH**

1 can (28 ounces) **PEELED, DICED TOMATOES**, including the juice

1½ cups sliced **OKRA**

1½ cups **FRESH CORN KERNELS** (from about 1 large ear of corn)

1 pound **ANDOUILLE SAUSAGE**, sliced

•• CONTINUED ••

In a large Dutch oven or other heavy-bottomed pot with a lid, sauté the bacon over medium heat, stirring frequently, for about 2 minutes until it just begins to render its fat. Add the onion, green pepper, garlic, and celery and sauté, stirring frequently, for about 10 minutes until the vegetables are tender. Drain any excess bacon fat.

Add the stock, tomatoes, okra, corn, and sausage. Bring to a simmer, partially cover the pot, and simmer for about 20 minutes until the okra is tender.

•• CONTINUED ••

2½ cups shredded **ROAST TURKEY**

½ cup chopped **FRESH FLAT-LEAF PARSLEY**

1 tablespoon minced **FRESH THYME**

1 teaspoon or more **TABASCO SAUCE**, or other hot sauce

KOSHER OR SEA SALT

1 tablespoon **FILÉ POWDER**

STEAMED WHITE RICE for serving

Stir in the turkey, ⅓ cup of the parsley, the thyme, and the Tabasco. Season to taste with salt. Remove from the heat and stir in the filé powder. (Do not allow the soup to boil once you have added the filé powder.)

To serve, spoon a mound of rice in the bottom of each of 8 warmed shallow bowls. Ladle the gumbo over top and garnish with the remaining parsley.

DO AHEAD   The gumbo, without the addition of the filé powder, can be made up to 2 days in advance, or frozen for up to 2 months. Cover and refrigerate until ready to reheat. Reheat the soup gently just before serving and then add the filé powder.

Classic Turkey Tetrazzini

Ah—turkey Tetrazzini—the homey casserole that turned into a cafeteria nightmare. Revive this classic for your family, but make it right! This casserole should be al dente spaghetti with a scattering of tender poultry and bright green peas, covered with a silken cream sauce and topped with crusty Parmesan bread crumbs. Serve it bubbly hot, straight from the oven.

2½ teaspoons **KOSHER OR SEA SALT**

12 ounces **SPAGHETTI**

6 tablespoons (¾ stick) **UNSALTED BUTTER**, plus extra for coating pans

6 tablespoons **ALL-PURPOSE FLOUR**

3½ cups **After-Thanksgiving Turkey Stock** (page 190) **OR CANNED LOW-SODIUM CHICKEN BROTH**

¾ cup **HEAVY (WHIPPING) CREAM**

1 tablespoon minced **FRESH THYME**

2 teaspoons minced **FRESH ROSEMARY**

¼ teaspoon freshly grated **NUTMEG**

¼ teaspoon freshly ground **PEPPER**

3½ cups diced **ROAST TURKEY** (½-inch dice)

10 ounces **FROZEN GREEN PEAS**, partially thawed

½ cup **PANKO** (Japanese bread crumbs) or other plain dried bread crumbs

½ cup (2 ounces) freshly grated **PARMESAN CHEESE**, preferably Parmigiano-Reggiano

Fill a stockpot two-thirds full of water, cover, and bring to a boil over high heat. Add 2 teaspoons of the salt. Add the spaghetti and cook for 8 to 10 minutes until al dente (cooked through, but still slightly chewy). Drain, rinse under cold running water, and set aside.

Preheat the oven to 375°F. Butter a 9-by-13-inch baking pan.

In a 10-inch sauté pan, melt the 6 tablespoons butter over medium heat. Add the flour and cook, stirring constantly, for about 2 minutes until faintly colored. Gradually whisk in the stock and continue to stir for 3 to 5 minutes until the sauce is smooth and thickened. Whisk in the cream. Add the remaining ½ teaspoon salt, the thyme, rosemary, nutmeg, and pepper. Stir in the turkey and peas, and cook until heated through. Taste and adjust the seasoning. Remove from the heat.

Transfer the spaghetti to the prepared dish, spreading it evenly. Spoon the turkey mixture over top. In a small bowl, combine the bread crumbs and cheese. Sprinkle evenly over the turkey mixture. Bake, uncovered, for about 20 minutes until heated through and bubbly. Preheat the broiler. Slip the casserole under the broiler and broil for about 4 minutes until the top is browned. Serve immediately.

DO AHEAD The casserole can be assembled without the cheese and bread crumb topping up to 1 day in advance. Cover and refrigerate. Remove from the refrigerator 45 minutes before baking. Scatter the bread crumb topping over top just before baking. Plan on 30 to 40 minutes until the casserole is heated through and bubbly.

Yankee Turkey Pot Pie

SERVES 6

Old-fashioned pot pies called for a deep baking dish lined with a baked pastry crust. The meat was added with herbs from the garden and cooked vegetables were blended in. Topped with more pastry, soda biscuits, or dumplings, the pie was baked to bubbly goodness. Here we update the recipe and make it quicker, using frozen puff pastry as a crisp topper to a luscious pot pie baked in a deep dish without the need for a pastry liner. Make individual servings in ramekins or ovenproof mugs, if desired.

1 sheet **FROZEN PUFF PASTRY DOUGH** (from a 17.3-ounce package)

1½ cups **After-Thanksgiving Turkey Stock** (page 190) **OR CANNED LOW-SODIUM CHICKEN BROTH**

1 large **CARROT**, peeled, halved lengthwise, and thinly sliced

3 tablespoons **UNSALTED BUTTER**

2 tablespoons **CANOLA OIL**

1 small **YELLOW ONION**, diced

8 ounces **CREMINI MUSHROOMS**, wiped or brushed clean and quartered

2 tablespoons **ALL-PURPOSE FLOUR**

½ cup **HEAVY (WHIPPING) CREAM**

3 cups diced **ROAST TURKEY** (½-inch dice)

½ cup finely chopped **FRESH FLAT-LEAF PARSLEY**

KOSHER OR SEA SALT

Freshly ground **PEPPER**

Remove 1 of the pastry sheets from the package and let thaw at room temperature for 30 minutes. Tightly seal the remaining pastry and freeze for another use.

Meanwhile, make the filling: Preheat the oven to 400°F. Have ready an 8-cup round baking dish about 2 inches deep, or use a 10-inch cast-iron skillet with 2-inch sides, and make the filling right in the skillet.

In a saucepan over medium heat, bring the stock to a boil. Add the carrot and cook for about 10 minutes until crisp-tender. Using a slotted spoon, transfer the carrot to a plate and set aside. Remove the stock from the heat and set aside.

In a 10-inch skillet, melt the butter with the oil over medium heat until the butter foams. Add the onion and sauté for about 2 minutes until it begins to soften. Add the mushrooms and sauté for about 3 minutes longer until they just begin to brown. Sprinkle the flour over the onion-mushroom mixture and stir to blend in. Slowly stir in the stock, bring to a simmer, and cook, stirring, for about 2 minutes until smooth and thickened. Add the cream, stir to blend, and bring to a simmer. Add the carrots, turkey, and parsley. Stir to combine. Return the mixture to a simmer, then season with salt and pepper to taste. Remove from the heat. Spoon the filling into the baking dish, or leave it in the cast iron skillet you cooked the filling in.

Unfold the sheet of puff pastry and lay it flat on a lightly floured work surface. Roll out the puff pastry to an 11-inch square, trimming the edges with a paring knife to form a circle. Cut three 2-inch-long slits in the center of the dough. Carefully place the dough over the filling, centering it. Firmly press the edges of the dough against the sides of the baking dish or cast iron skillet. Bake for about 25 minutes until the dough is nicely browned and puffed. Serve immediately.

Turkey Enchiladas with Creamy Tomatillo Sauce

SERVES 4   If you have grill-roasted your turkey, then make this recipe as a way to deliciously use up the turkey leftovers. The smoky flavor of the meat accents the creamy tomatillo sauce.

2 cups shredded **ROAST TURKEY**

2 **GREEN ONIONS**, including tender green tops, thinly sliced

3 tablespoons **CREAM CHEESE** at room temperature

1⅓ cups (5½ ounces) shredded **MONTEREY JACK CHEESE**

2 cans (7 ounces each) **SALSA VERDE**, or 1 can (13 ounces) **TOMATILLOS**, drained

2 tablespoons canned **CHOPPED GREEN CHILES**, drained

½ cup **FRESH CILANTRO LEAVES**

⅔ cup **HEAVY (WHIPPING) CREAM**

¼ cup **CANOLA OIL**

8 **CORN TORTILLAS**

Preheat the oven to 350°F. In a medium bowl, combine the turkey, green onions, cream cheese, and 1 cup of jack cheese and stir to mix thoroughly. Set aside.

In a blender or food processor, combine the salsa verde, chiles, cilantro, and cream and process until smooth.

Heat the oil in a heavy, 6-inch skillet over medium-high heat. Using tongs, carefully place 1 tortilla at a time in the hot oil and fry for 5 to 10 seconds just until softened. Flip the tortilla and soften the other side. Drain over the skillet, then place on a plate lined with a paper towel. Place another paper towel on top and press to absorb the oil. Repeat until all 8 tortillas are softened and drained.

Divide the turkey mixture among the tortillas (about ½ cup each), mounding it in a line down the center. Roll tightly and place, seam side down, in a 7-by-11-inch baking pan. Pour the tomatillo-cream sauce over the enchiladas, and sprinkle the remaining ⅓ cup jack cheese down the center. Bake for about 20 minutes until heated through and bubbly. Serve immediately.

DO AHEAD   The enchiladas can be made up to 1 day in advance. Cover and refrigerate. Remove from the refrigerator 45 minutes before baking. Plan on 30 to 35 minutes until the casserole is heated through and bubbly.

David's Killer Day-of-the-Bird Turkey Sandwich

SERVES 1

For this recipe, I must give credit to David Saffer, the fine husband of my literary agent, Lisa Ekus-Saffer. "Day of the Bird" refers to the fact that this sandwich is meant to be eaten on Thanksgiving night, not the day or two following. It is for true "turkey-aholics," those who just cannot get enough of the bird during the main meal because of all those pesky side dishes. According to David, this sandwich tastes best when eaten over the kitchen sink and no sooner than four hours after the meal.

2 slices **RYE BREAD** (preferably with seeds), or other favorite sandwich bread

BROWN MUSTARD

LEFTOVER TURKEY, white and dark meat

LEFTOVER DRESSING

LEFTOVER CRANBERRY SAUCE (optional)

Spread 1 slice of the bread with a generous amount of mustard. Layer with turkey meat, dressing, and cranberry sauce, if using. Top with the second slice of bread and press gently. Do not cut in half.

Lean over the countertop or sink and eat immediately.

COOK'S NOTE

Some turkey-aholics prefer a simple horseradish sauce. Combine 2 parts mayonnaise with 1 part bottled horseradish and mix well.

Regional Thanksgiving Menus with Timetables

Thanksgiving a moveable feast? In 1863, in response to the tireless campaign of magazine editor Sarah Hale, President Abraham Lincoln proclaimed the last Thursday in November an annual, national day of thanksgiving. This lasted until 1939, when retailers persuaded President Franklin Roosevelt to move the date up to increase the shopping days to Christmas: twenty-three states agreed, twenty-three states observed the original date, and two states—Colorado and Texas—celebrated both! The muddle continued that next year, prompting Congress in 1941 to set Thanksgiving on the fourth Thursday of November. Now, whether you're planning a Heartland Thanksgiving or a menu from the Pacific Northwest, rest assured that all Americans are celebrating on the same day (I hope!).

Planning Tips for Thanksgiving

LISTS, LISTS, AND MORE LISTS The first thing I do when planning my Thanksgiving dinner—actually the entire weekend, since we usually have out-of-town guests—is to make lists. I begin with a list of my invited guests and make notes detailing whether they will be joining us only for the big meal or staying all or part of the weekend. I make another list with the menu for each meal, but obviously the big Thanksgiving dinner gets the most detailed attention. I start building two different grocery lists: one has all the staples and nonperishables; the other list has the produce, dairy, meats, and breads that I need to buy a few days ahead. Finally, I write to-do lists for each day. This includes the recipes I plan to make ahead, the errands I need to run, and so on. For me, this makes the holiday weekend more relaxed because I have a strategy and game plan. I'm lined up and ready to tackle, just like all the football players on TV Thanksgiving weekend!

THE OVERALL STRATEGY This dovetails with making lists. If I plan the guest list, decide on the menu, plan the wine and other beverages to be served, and plan how my table is going to look—including whether serving family-style or buffet-style makes more sense—then I can visualize and think through my needs. The most important strategic question is whether you are cooking everything yourself or handing out cooking assignments. My philosophy is that Thanksgiving is about family and friends sharing time and giving thanks. So, as the host, put yourself in a thankful frame of mind for the many hands that can make the day easier and more relaxed. Don't be shy—hand out cooking assignments and ask others who don't cook to contribute wine and beverages.

THE TURKEY Remember to order your turkey 2 weeks in advance so you get the size and type of turkey you want. If you plan to brine, follow the brining schedule outlined on page 71. You'll need to have a fresh or thawed turkey ready to brine on the Tuesday before Thanksgiving. I pick up my fresh turkey on either Sunday or Monday, depending on my work schedule. This way I can brine it Tuesday afternoon or evening. Remember that fresh birds are commercially refrigerated just above freezing, which means they often have icy juices in the chest cavity. A day or two in a home refrigerator eliminates the problem.

A WELL-STOCKED PANTRY To simplify shopping and minimize the number of trips to the supermarket and specialty food stores, take stock of what is in your pantry and stock up on staples such as oils and vinegars, sugars and flours, herbs and spices, canned tomatoes, beans, and canned broths. If your herbs and spices are old then this is the time to replace them with fresh ones.

Even if you're not hosting out-of-town guests, you never know when Thanksgiving visiting and feasting may start in the days before or extend into the weekend. This is why a clever host keeps jars of olives, pickles, tapenade, and other delectable nibbles and spreads on the pantry shelf during the holidays for spur-of-the-moment entertaining and in-between meal snacks. Containers of nuts and boxes of best-quality crackers, chips, and bread sticks make it easy to assemble party hors d'oeuvres and appetizers without a lot of fuss. Stock your refrigerator with interesting cheeses as well as ready-to-eat crudités such as baby carrots, radishes, and celery hearts.

KITCHEN EQUIPMENT Once you have decided on the Thanksgiving menu (and any weekend meals you may be preparing), inventory your kitchen and determine whether you have all the pots, sauté pans, roasting pans, and other equipment you'll need to make the recipes. Invest in equipment you'll use again and again. For specialty items or recipes you don't think you'll turn to often, remember you can always borrow from friends. A Bundt pan, for instance, is called for to make the terrific, do-ahead Molasses Gingerbread Cake with Cinnamon Whipped Cream on page 175. Make and freeze the cake 3 weeks ahead, and return the pan well before your friend will be looking for it during the holidays. I like to invest in well-made equipment and pans, which means buying slowly, waiting until I can afford top-quality items.

TABLEWARE AND DÉCOR The biggest lesson I have learned from years of entertaining is to check my linens, dishware, and glassware well ahead of my party to make sure I have enough of everything I need. In addition, I always set my table the day before my party. (It never fails—every time I feel harried when entertaining, it's because I didn't get the table set the night before—especially for Thanksgiving!) While you are thinking about your tableware, think about your table décor and whether you are going to buy flowers and arrange a centerpiece yourself, or order one from a florist, or create a contemporary look with several candles or votives placed down the length of the table with, perhaps, an arrangement of squashes and gourds, intermixed.

Delicious food and beautiful tableware go hand-in-hand; so does hot food and warm plates. You can warm your dinner plates in a clean dishwasher set on the dry cycle. Some dishwashers even have a plate-warming feature. Or, run the plates under very hot water, dry them, and wrap them in a terry towel until needed. For those with a plate-warming drawer—lucky you! Do not heat plates in the oven; good china can crack from the thermal change, and, besides, the oven will most likely still be busy with warming side dishes.

WINE AND BEVERAGES Organize and plan what you will be serving. Refrigerate white wines, sparkling wines, and beer, as well as soft drinks and juices, in time to get them well chilled. Uncork or decant red wines that need breathing before guests arrive. Consider serving children apple juice or sparkling apple cider in short-stemmed glasses to include them in the pomp of the holiday table; it makes them feel grown-up and special. If you are planning to serve coffee and tea, measure the coffee ahead of time. Thermal serving carafes are convenient, especially if you set up a dessert buffet.

Thanksgiving Dinner in New England

New Englanders, intellectual and of sturdy stock and sound conscience, didn't have to look far for their main sustenance because the fertile land and abundant waters provided a diet rich in corn, beans, fish, seafood, wild game and fowl, fruit, berries, and maple syrup. The first Thanksgiving at Plymouth, celebrated with the Wampanoag Indians in 1621, reflected this abundance. It is said that the Pilgrims might not have survived the first harsh winter had it not been for the endless supply of mussels along the shore. It seems fitting that this Thanksgiving menu reflects the glorious traditions and bounty of the six New England states. It was hard to decide which pies to put on this menu, so I've included two. After all, New England is known as the Pie Belt, and when a Down-Easter anticipates pie he loosens the buckle on his belt a notch.

3 WEEKS AHEAD
- Plan your menu.
- Make two grocery lists, separating staples from perishables.
- Select wine and other beverages.
- Check your kitchen tools and equipment.
- Plan your table setting and décor; check serving platters, bowls, and utensils.

2 WEEKS AHEAD
- Order a fresh turkey.
- Make the gingerbread cake and freeze.
- Make the pastry dough for one or both pies and freeze.
- Make a big batch of turkey stock, if desired, and freeze.

1 WEEK AHEAD
- Make the cranberry compote and refrigerate.

3 DAYS AHEAD
- Make the cheddar cheese straws and store at room temperature.
- Make the apple cider brine and refrigerate.
- Make the bread cubes for the stuffing and store at room temperature.

2 DAYS AHEAD
- Brine the turkey.
- Make the turkey stock for gravy and refrigerate.
- Thaw the pastry dough for the pies in the refrigerator.

1 DAY AHEAD
- Make the gravy and refrigerate.
- Remove the turkey from the brine, rinse, pat dry, and refrigerate, uncovered.
- Sauté the vegetables and herbs for the stuffing and refrigerate.
- Make the sweet potatoes and refrigerate.
- Buy Parker House rolls.
- Thaw gingerbread cake, if serving.

THANKSGIVING MORNING
- Refresh the cheddar cheese straws and arrange them for serving.
- Peel and cut the potatoes; place in a pan with cold water to cover. Set aside.
- Prepare all the vegetables for the succotash and set aside.
- Assemble and bake one or two pies.

5 HOURS AHEAD
- Remove the turkey from the refrigerator and prepare for roasting.
- Measure the ingredients for the oyster stew and refrigerate.
- Whip the cream for the desserts.

3½ HOURS AHEAD
- Roast the turkey.

2 HOURS AHEAD
- Arrange the relish tray and pickled vegetables.
- Remove the vegetables for the stuffing from the refrigerator. Assemble the stuffing.
- Remove the sweet potatoes from the refrigerator.

1 HOUR AHEAD
- Make the oyster stew and keep warm.
- Make the mashed potatoes and keep warm.
- Put the cranberry compote in a serving dish.
- Bake the stuffing.

SHORTLY BEFORE SERVING
- Heat the sweet potatoes.
- Heat the gravy and keep warm.
- Sauté the succotash.
- Warm the dinner rolls.

A Heartland Thanksgiving

Some might say it's not Thanksgiving in the Midwest without a turkey in the fryer (or a turkey-fryer fire). This menu keeps safety in mind as you roast a classically seasoned, plump and perky bird with delicious results. With long stretches of grasslands and abundant lakes, orchards, and farms, the Midwest, called the Breadbasket of America, has a tradition of simple and hearty fare. Make classic deviled eggs as a nod to Indiana, the leader in egg production. Be thankful for the lush wheat fields of Kansas and bake a loaf of Heartland Cottage Cheese Dill Bread. A meal in the Midwest wouldn't be complete without bread on the table. Stay with tradition and make a classic molded gelatin salad, but follow my lead and update the green bean casserole with my Green Beans with Lemon-Butter Bread Crumbs and Toasted Almonds. Save room for irresistible persimmon pudding—another Indiana favorite.

Classic deviled eggs

Butter pickles, corn relish, celery sticks, and baby carrots

3 WEEKS AHEAD
- Plan your menu.
- Make two grocery lists, separating staples from perishables.
- Select wine and other beverages.
- Check your kitchen tools and equipment.
- Plan your table setting and décor, check serving platters, bowls, and utensils.

2 WEEKS AHEAD
- Order a fresh turkey.
- Make the pastry dough for the pies and freeze.
- Make a big batch of turkey stock, if desired, and freeze.

3 DAYS AHEAD
- Boil the eggs for the deviled eggs and refrigerate.
- Make the parsnip soup and refrigerate.
- Make the juniper brine and store at room temperature.
- Make the cranberry compote and refrigerate.

2 DAYS AHEAD
- Brine the turkey.
- Make the turkey stock for gravy and refrigerate.
- Thaw the pastry dough for the pies in the refrigerator.

1 DAY AHEAD
- Peel, halve, and make the filling for the deviled eggs and refrigerate.
- Make the bacon garnish for the soup and refrigerate.
- Make the cottage cheese dill bread and store at room temperature.
- Make the gravy and refrigerate.
- Remove the turkey from the brine, rinse, pat dry, and refrigerate uncovered.
- Make the wild rice dressing and refrigerate.
- Make the sweet potatoes and refrigerate.
- Blanch the pearl onions and refrigerate.
- Make the filling for the pumpkin pies.

THANKSGIVING MORNING
- Peel and cut the potatoes; place in a pan with cold water to cover. Set aside.
- Assemble and bake the pies.
- Make the persimmon pudding.
- Blanch the green beans and set aside.
- Toast the almonds and make the bread crumb topping for the green beans.

5 HOURS AHEAD
- Remove the turkey from the refrigerator and prepare for roasting.
- Whip the cream for the desserts.

3½ HOURS AHEAD
- Roast the turkey.
- Assemble and garnish the deviled eggs. Cover and refrigerate.

2 HOURS AHEAD
- Arrange an appetizer tray with the pickles, corn relish, and fresh vegetables.
- Remove the wild rice dressing, sweet potatoes, and pearl onions from the refrigerator.

1 HOUR AHEAD
- Heat the wild rice dressing.
- Make the mashed potatoes and keep warm.
- Make the creamed onions and keep warm.
- Put the cranberry compote in a serving dish.

SHORTLY BEFORE SERVING
- Heat the soup.
- Heat the sweet potatoes.
- Crisp the bacon garnish for the soup.
- Warm the bread and slice it.
- Heat the gravy and keep warm.
- Finish assembly of the green beans.

Southern Style—Thanksgiving Dinner for a Dozen

Creating a definitive Southern Thanksgiving is impossible, because as you travel state to state the glorious traditions vary. In North Carolina, it's likely a ham is roasting alongside a plump turkey and the natural pan juices are turned into creamy onion gravy. In Georgia, collard greens are simmered with bits of ham, and butterbeans are stewed, along with tomatoes. Corn is creamed or made into fritters. Potatoes might be served as potato salad rather than mashed. Head to Louisiana and find yourself nibbling on oysters to start and then tucking into a turducken as the centerpiece of the meal. This menu captures the flavors and foods of the region. Add your family favorites, but don't forget freshly baked biscuits and a pitcher of iced tea—the wine of the South.

3 WEEKS AHEAD
- Plan your menu.
- Make two grocery lists, separating staples from perishables.
- Select wine and other beverages.
- Check your kitchen tools and equipment.
- Plan your table setting and décor, check serving platters, bowls, and utensils.

2 WEEKS AHEAD
- Order a fresh turkey.
- Make the pastry dough for the pies and freeze.
- Make a big batch of turkey stock, if desired, and freeze.

1 WEEK AHEAD
- Make the cranberry compote and refrigerate.

3 DAYS AHEAD
- Make the honey and allspice brine and store at room temperature.
- Make the bread cubes for the stuffing and store at room temperature.

2 DAYS AHEAD
- Brine the turkey.
- Make the turkey stock for gravy and refrigerate.
- Thaw the pastry dough for the pies in the refrigerator.

1 DAY AHEAD
- Make the crostini and shrimp.
- Wash the salad greens and refrigerate. Toast the pecans for the salad. Make the salad dressing and refrigerate.
- Remove the turkey from the brine, rinse, pat dry, and refrigerate uncovered.
- Make the gravy and refrigerate.
- Make the cornbread and store at room temperature.
- Make the key lime tart and refrigerate.
- Make the sweet potatoes and topping and store in the refrigerator.
- Blanch the pearl onions and refrigerate.

THANKSGIVING MORNING
- Make the pecan pie.
- Assemble the stuffing and refrigerate.
- Peel and cut the potatoes; place in a pan with cold water to cover. Set aside.
- Chop and assemble the ingredients for the Brussels sprouts.

5 HOURS AHEAD
- Remove the turkey from the refrigerator and prepare for roasting.
- Whip the cream for the pie.

3½ HOURS AHEAD
- Roast the turkey.
- Put the nuts in bowls.

2 HOURS AHEAD
- Remove the stuffing and the sweet potatoes and topping from the refrigerator.
- Remove the pearl onions from the refrigerator.
- Make the biscuits.

1 HOUR AHEAD
- Assemble the shrimp appetizers.
- Remove the salad dressing from the refrigerator.
- Put the cranberry compote in a serving dish.
- Bake the stuffing.
- Assemble and bake the sweet potatoes.
- Make the mashed potatoes and keep warm.
- Make the creamed onions and keep warm.

SHORTLY BEFORE SERVING
- Heat the gravy and keep warm.
- Cut the pears and toss the salad.
- Sauté the Brussels sprouts.
- Warm the biscuits.

A Bountiful Thanksgiving in the Pacific Northwest

This menu captures the glorious food history of the Pacific Northwest, evolving from the Native Americans who enjoyed the bounty from both land and sea. In 1805, Lewis and Clark, along with a large scouting party, wintered over at Fort Clatsop on the Oregon Coast. Though, surprisingly, they did not favor the fresh salmon offered by the Indians, they did embrace the beauty of the region and relished the northwest's authentic and traditional foods. From our long coastline and mighty rivers we enjoy salmon; cranberries are gathered from the coastal bogs; from our damp forests we gather wild mushrooms, such as the chanterelles used in the gravy. Pears, hazelnuts, chestnuts, and apples are all harvested from northwest orchards. Our farmland is fertile, providing seasonal, local produce year-round. Boutique creameries make splendid cheeses and, of course, our wineries are world renowned. Serve a rich Oregon Pinot Noir, ideal with this festive meal.

3 WEEKS AHEAD
- Plan your menu.
- Make two grocery lists, separating staples from perishables.
- Select wine and other beverages.
- Check your kitchen tools and equipment.
- Plan your table setting and décor, check serving platters, bowls, and utensils.

2 WEEKS AHEAD
- Order a fresh turkey.
- Make the pumpkin cake and frosting. Assemble the cake and freeze.
- Make a big batch of turkey stock, if desired, and freeze.
- Roast the chestnuts for the stuffing and freeze.

1 WEEK AHEAD
- Make the cranberry sauce and refrigerate.

3 DAYS AHEAD
- Boil the eggs for the deviled eggs and refrigerate.
- Make the juniper brine and store at room temperature.
- Make the bread cubes for the stuffing and store at room temperature.

2 DAYS AHEAD
- Brine the turkey.
- Make the turkey stock for gravy and refrigerate.
- Make the appetizer blue cheese spread and refrigerate.

1 DAY AHEAD
- Peel, halve, and make the filling for the deviled eggs and refrigerate.
- Thaw the cake in the refrigerator.
- Thaw the chestnuts and refresh them in the oven.
- Sauté the vegetables, apples, and herbs for the stuffing and refrigerate.
- Make the puff pastry wafers and store at room temperature.
- Make the gravy and refrigerate.
- Remove the turkey from the brine, rinse, pat dry, and refrigerate uncovered.
- Roast the carrots and parsnips and refrigerate.
- Make the sweet potatoes and topping and store in the refrigerator.
- Make the salad dressing and refrigerate.

THANKSGIVING MORNING
- Make the roasted pears and set aside at room temperature.
- Blanch the green beans and set aside.
- Toast the almonds and make the bread crumb topping for the green beans.
- Peel and cut the potatoes; place in a pan with cold water to cover. Set aside.
- Roast the hazelnuts for the salad and set aside.

5 HOURS AHEAD
- Remove the turkey from the refrigerator and prepare for roasting.

3½ HOURS AHEAD
- Roast the turkey.
- Assemble and garnish the deviled eggs. Cover and refrigerate.

2 HOURS AHEAD
- Make the batter for the popovers and set aside at room temperature.
- Remove the parsnips and carrots from the refrigerator.
- Remove the sweet potatoes and its topping from the refrigerator.
- Remove the vegetables for the stuffing from the refrigerator. Assemble the stuffing.
- Remove the salad dressing from the refrigerator.
- Toss the cranberries for the salad with dressing and set aside.
- Prepare the onions for the salad and set aside.
- Remove the blue cheese spread from the refrigerator.

1 HOUR AHEAD
- Bake the stuffing.
- Assemble and bake the sweet potatoes.
- Make the mashed potatoes and keep warm.
- Put the cranberry sauce in a serving dish.
- Heat the carrots and parsnips.
- Pipe the blue cheese spread on the puff pastry wafers and arrange on a serving plate. Remove the celery crudités from the refrigerator and arrange in a glass or narrow bowl.

SHORTLY BEFORE SERVING
- Bake the popovers.
- Heat the gravy and keep warm.
- Finish assembly of the green beans.
- Cut the pears and toss the salad.
- Remove the pumpkin cake from the refrigerator.
- Reheat the roasted pears.

Index

Table of Equivalents

The exact equivalents in the following tables have been rounded for convenience.

Liquid/Dry Measurements

U.S.	METRIC
¼ teaspoon	1.25 milliliters
½ teaspoon	2.5 milliliters
1 teaspoon	5 milliliters
1 tablespoon (3 teaspoons)	15 milliliters
1 fluid ounce (2 tablespoons)	30 milliliters
¼ cup	60 milliliters
⅓ cup	80 milliliters
½ cup	120 milliliters
1 cup	240 milliliters
1 pint (2 cups)	480 milliliters
1 quart (4 cups, 32 ounces)	960 milliliters
1 gallon (4 quarts)	3.84 liters
1 ounce (by weight)	28 grams
1 pound	448 grams
2.2 pounds	1 kilogram

Lengths

U.S.	METRIC
⅛ inch	3 millimeters
¼ inch	6 millimeters
½ inch	12 millimeters
1 inch	2.5 centimeters

Oven Temperature

FAHRENHEIT	CELSIUS	GAS
250	120	½
275	140	1
300	150	2
325	160	3
350	180	4
375	190	5
400	200	6
425	220	7
450	230	8
475	240	9
500	260	10